R. H. Mansfield is an educator at a school for students with Autism. She resides with her husband, two adult children, and two cats. Prior to their trek to Florida, Mansfield was a Kentuckian who made her way to the interior and Southeast Alaska as an educator for almost a decade, working as a special educator and English teacher. Mansfield and her family regularly enjoy beach time, traveling, and board games.

To my loving family who inspire me every day with their innate goodness, love, and support.

To my chosen family, Christopher and Jessica, who throughout my life have been there for me and somehow still love me unconditionally, even when I did not love myself.

R.H. Mansfield

RAISED BY CHILDREN

AUSTIN MACAULEY PUBLISHERS
LONDON * CAMBRIDGE * NEW YORK * SHARJAH

Copyright © R.H. Mansfield 2025

All rights reserved. No part of this publication may be reproduced, distributed, or transmitted in any form or by any means, including photocopying, recording, or other electronic or mechanical methods, without the prior written permission of the publisher, except in the case of brief quotations embodied in critical reviews and certain other non-commercial uses permitted by copyright law. For permission requests, write to the publisher.

Any person who commits any unauthorized act in relation to this publication may be liable to criminal prosecution and civil claims for damages.

All of the events in this memoir are true to the best of author's memory. The views expressed in this memoir are solely those of the author.

Ordering Information
Quantity sales: Special discounts are available on quantity purchases by corporations, associations, and others. For details, contact the publisher at the address below.

Publisher's Cataloging-in-Publication data
Mansfield, R.H.
Raised by Children

ISBN 9798895430163 (Paperback)
ISBN 9798895430170 (Hardback)
ISBN 9798895430187 (ePub e-book)

Library of Congress Control Number: 2025905394

www.austinmacauley.com/us

First Published 2025
Austin Macauley Publishers LLC
40 Wall Street, 33rd Floor, Suite 3302
New York, NY 10005
USA

mail-usa@austinmacauley.com
+1 (646) 5125767

Table of Contents

Happy Birthday	**9**
Grams	**19**
My Favorite Doll and the Television	**22**
The Evil Queen and the Red-Headed Stepchild	**33**
Square Peg in a Round Hole	**54**
The Road Not Taken	**62**
Motherhood	**70**
Ungrateful	**81**
My Vulcan Baby	**98**
Because Mars Wasn't Hiring	**99**

Happy Birthday

My mom was 14 and pregnant when she married my 19-year-old dad after he failed his first college semester. I often wondered how my dad could have loved my mom as a 14-year-old girl, so young and in junior high school. I teach freshmen, and I see my mom in those tiny developing faces.

I wonder if girls my dad's age could see through his bullshit and if he needed a young child to groom and control. At the time, pregnant girls didn't finish school due to lack of options. They were just thrown out.

My mom ended up finishing school through a correspondence course while she raised toddlers. Every three years, she had a new baby. I remember the story she would tell about dragging me to school at four and pleading with them to take me early because I would be turning five within the month.

My husband Hilary points out that sometimes my funny stories about my crazy family are not ironic or funny but show a sad sense of tragedy. More often than not, he is right, but I have internalized this reality to the point that it just *is*. It is not sad or happy. It just *is*.

My fifth birthday is one of those stories.

My mother left on my fifth birthday, but I do not remember it as the day she left. I remember it as a bright sunny day for a trip to the zoo. I don't know whether I realized she wasn't simply at work or that she wasn't coming back.

It took a while to realize the ramifications of the full situation. No adults sat me down to explain. It just happened, and we were all supposed to act like everything was normal. I remember feeling this emptiness though.

When I put it together late one night, my two older sisters and I were waiting for Dad to get back from work. We were stirring a big pot of macaroni and cheese on the stove. We'd take turns stirring, and I had a stool to stand on to get me to the height of the stove.

I can still feel the steam from the pot as I held the big wooden spoon. My dad had a fairly long commute, so my sisters handled most everything else at the house. Unfortunately, with my mother gone, Summer, my oldest sister who would be roughly 11 years old by this time, became the new person to yell at for all problems in the house, like the water heater breaking.

When our water heater went out, my dad would boil water in a big spaghetti pot for our baths.

I remember sitting in this dark house saying, "I want to go home. I want to go home."

I didn't understand the feeling exactly, other than this simply wasn't home anymore. The house was dark, and the long living room felt like a chasm. I stood in the entrance hallway, looking out the glass panel door.

Summer said, "Stop saying that. You'll hurt Dad's feelings."

And there it was. The biggest concern. Let's not hurt Dad's feelings. My sister. Always the parent.

One of my oldest memories was watching my dad jump up from his seat, scoop up my mother off the couch, walk out the front door, down the three steps of the porch, and throw her in the front yard.

She was wearing a yellow sweatshirt with Garfield eating a slice of pizza on it. I walked to the door, wondering what I was looking at, clearly not perceiving the situation for what it was.

For what purpose she was thrown, I will never know.

When I got older around 11 or 12, I told my dad this memory. He said that since I put my mom on such a high pedestal, it was my fault I recalled the events in this way and omitted all the bad things my mom did, hurting his feelings which was something we were never to do. His feelings took precedence. She evidently threw plates during arguments.

It was an odd accusation because I did not know my mother well enough to put her on a pedestal. Honestly, I wasn't sure if I liked her all that much. She seemed to have very little interest in me.

By the time I was 11, my sisters both lived with her now, and they seemed, as they always have, to be raising themselves. My mother did not seem to want us until we could fend for ourselves, and that child tax credit was capped after two children.

Later in adult life, the concern about other people's feelings still takes precedence over my feelings. So much so, that in situations where I draw boundaries and indicate behaviors I will not tolerate, I feel bad for standing up for myself. I will feel bad for how I make others feel who are actively hurting me when I have every right to say stop.

Another early memory is sitting in the car looking out the windows. I remember lots of times waiting in cars and lots of commuting back and forth. I remember watching the wheels turning.

The back tires of the semi on the interstate were about eye level with me. The wheels turned faster and faster, but rhythmically. I remember staring into it like a trance and thinking about how a quick veer of the car would crush me between the wheels.

Commuting sucked! It always caused fights. I would fantasize about having teleportation powers. That way, I didn't have to hear them complain about each other, complain about me.

My mom would play little games with custody agreements too in order to get her way.

She would ask my dad to meet her halfway, then not go. She would say she never found him, so, he had to come and get us.

She would agree that he could drop us off at her house, and she would bring us back, but then she would refuse to bring us back at all, saying, "If you want them, come and get them."

Once, she refused to let us leave because he came too late, and she didn't want us to travel after midnight. Since she worked nights, we had to hear my dad's incessant answering machine messages about how we needed to just come outside and come home with him, knowing we were told not to do so.

It was painful, the pleading from each parent to do as we were told but the instructions were the opposite. Once, my mom refused to have me leave after the summer, and the cops were called and forced me to leave with my dad as determined by their custody agreement.

Long boring summers spent at my mom's and Stephen's house were tough because I didn't have my stuff, my friends, or much of anything. I tried to bring my drum set, but instead of being on board with the idea, my dad demanded my mom pay him for my things.

He even tried to insist that, in the custody agreement, Grams, Stephen's mother, had no right to spend time with me, so he would try to take it away but was unsuccessful.

Before she switched to the day shift, my mom worked long hours and slept throughout the day, so my summers would be spent with 'Saved by the Bell', 'Wings', 'Designing Women', and some scandalous talk shows.

My connection to the outside world I found through letters with my best friend, Jessie, a connection that kept me sane and continues to keep me sane. We'd email and write physical letters. I would send her pressed four-leaf clovers that Stephen planted around the koi pond.

I would get in trouble for using up all the office supplies crafting and boxes of matches. I liked lighting one match and watching the whole pack catch on fire with a fun pop and intoxicating smell, reminiscent of campfires.

Once, Grams took me to Dee's Crafts and bought me a craft book on how to make wooden dowel finger puppets and supplies which kept me occupied all summer long. I would create fairy tale plays with princes, princesses, vampires, and animal characters. Grams always found a way to encourage creativity and curiosity. She taught me the world was bigger than the corner I inhabited.

Another early memory was nothing more than an image. I watched the car turn in a large roundabout that surrounded the Nelson County Courthouse in the historic district of downtown Bardstown.

It was a beautiful humongous building, and the cars seemed to dance around. A roundabout was weird to watch. The directions of the cars did not make sense.

"That is the courthouse," someone in the car told me.

Courthouse? Court? Lawyers? I knew a friend whose parents separated and eventually divorced. I remember- I was still about five years old thinking about the ramifications of my mother leaving—thinking divorce? My parents will probably get a divorce. They should get a divorce. They seem to hate each other.

I wasn't like many kids whose parents got divorced. Many wanted their parents to get back together, but I never felt this way. I remember Thanksgiving when Autumn and I broke the wishbone. I held the longest piece triumphantly, but Autumn badgered me for what I wished for, and it seemed rather important to her.

I told her I wished for She-Ra to be real. She-Ra was an amazing woman with big beautiful flowing long hair who had both the strength and virtue to know what to do to help everyone. I believe she could save the world. She would empower the rebels to stand up for themselves instead of waiting for her to save them. After the show,

Loo-Kee, who hid in the background of the episode, would jump out of the picture and talk to me directly and share whatever social story that could be derived from the episode.

Autumn glared at me disappointedly and said, "I wanted Mom and Dad back together."

I was embarrassed that she didn't win, that I didn't think to answer this way, and more importantly, that I did not want that. It sounded horrible. I would rather have She-Ra than the two parts together that did not fit.

Not long after my mom left, my dad was taking us somewhere. I forget where, but that wasn't important. I saw my dad whip the steering wheel quickly like he did when he scooped my mom off the couch and dropped him in the front yard.

He spun the truck into the KFC parking lot and parked. My mom was eating with a man, Stephen, my mom's boyfriend whom she later married.

My dad starts gesturing wildly and screaming, "This is what your mom does. This is how she spends my money. This is why she left you. She doesn't care."

His rambling continued but I couldn't hear what followed because the three of us were in tears and wailing. My mom looked sick, and Stephen left to get a manager. By the time the manager became visible, my dad drove off. The damage was done.

My dad became all Emo for a bit and played Cathy's 'Clown' and 'You Chose a Fine Time to Leave Me' by Lucille, songs victimizing the cuckolded male and portraying the woman as selfish.

This particular image would creep up on me often as I got older. Once, when I was trick-or-treating with a friend, I told my friend and her mother what happened. I think someone mentioned KFC or something. They all looked at me mortified, and I apologized for not realizing this wasn't an interesting story.

The story came to mind again once when I was in high school. My dad was taking a writing course, for some reason, and he came home enraged because some little twit in his class discussed how divorced parents use their kids to hurt each other.

Since my dad did not react well to the story about my remembering how he threw my mom in the front yard, I imagine he would not appreciate an example of how he used us to hurt my mother that day, screaming about how she was spending his money in the KFC parking lot.

The first time my mom came to get us for a visitation, she pulled up the long gravel driveway with Stephen. There was no legal precedent that said Stephen could not be in the car, and based on my dad's behavior, I truly think my mom was scared of him. We were pretty scared of him.

I hadn't seen my mom in a while, and I was eager to know if she still loved me. Our elementary class had a Read With A Parent Day, and I was embarrassed because everyone's mom came in to read with them, but my aunt showed up.

I thought my dad told my mom, but she didn't come. I thought she was mad at me or just didn't want to see me. I remember seeing Sissy, my aunt, on a cold morning with her bright red nose staring back, eager to help me. But she wasn't who I was looking for, and I did not like Sissy.

My dad refused to let us leave with my mom and started yelling at her that Stephen was not to go on his property. He should have been dropped off at the end of the driveway, blah, blah, blah.

"Can we just go," I yelled. Everyone stopped and stared at me.

"Can we just go," I yelled again crying, looking up at everyone staring down at me standing on the sidewalk lined with yellow tulips my mom had planted earlier that spring.

I was so tiny, but somehow everything stopped, and we left. All the arguments, all the property discussions melted away and for a moment, just a moment, they all saw me and what they were doing in a physically tangible way like the very property we stood upon, falling around me like ripped-up pieces of paper.

It would be wrong of me to blame her for leaving on my birthday. My dad picked the date. It was a painful date to choose, which was his intention, and it was his doing. My birthday was not a story of a woman abandoning her children.

It was a story of a woman, groomed as a child, making an escape the only way she could, at the expense of her children, to get away from a very controlling man. But it was a story of freedom, nonetheless.

Happy Birthday

I've always liked the zoo.
Riding camels
And watching the white polar
bears Flat in blue waters
From the side window.

I remember watching
elephants Spray their trunks
in the air Reminiscent of that
Sesame Street scene.
Where the elephant dances
To the song Splish Splash.

I remember the orange
Orangutan Like Caesar.
Knock on the glass

To get my toddler's attention
From the stroller.

I remember school field trips
and research projects about
the banded linsang

And the tiny monkey behind
the glass

Like he climbed from the
pages of Curious George
Zoos are fun.
I like animals.

Once my mom left
On my birthday
While we were at the zoo.
I carried around a little
plastic snail. It was a great
day.
I was five.

It is a tragic startling story
for people.
But I still like the zoo.
And my birthday.

But I still like the zoo,
And my birthday

And never remembering
thinking it was
All that bad.

But the story startles people
like something that should be
tragic.

Grams

Evidently, since my mom hated the drive so horribly, I would be pawned off to Grams.

She would drive to school on Monday mornings after every other weekend without being resentful with her time. It was a long commute, and we would talk or sing the whole way. She'd buy me books or talk about books.

In fifth grade, we read 'The Secret Garden' and while I loved the book, it was Grams who helped me understand the British Imperialism of India found in Mary Lennox's and her family's backstory, bringing importance to the ivory elephants held by the twin sisters.

Arguably, this book read in elementary school led me to my love of British Literature, later resulting in my first master's degree.

She took me to the movies like 'Evita' and explained all the history I didn't follow, specifically how Evita was not an empowering woman wanting to better the world. She wanted to overthrow the aristocracy who treated her poorly because she was poor.

She didn't want to create a rise of the proletariat. She wanted to be queen or at least look like one and be above those who subjugated her. Her actions were done for show as illustrated by the lines of children circling the town, waiting for their new shoes. We would bond over a viewing of Braveheart, and the slight glimpse of Mel Gibson's butt.

She took me to other worlds through books and theater. We traveled to Hawaii and Antarctica at the IMAX. In Antarctica, the camera work would go into the water, and the penguins diving into the icy blue abyss turned into acrobats playing inside a pink and blue light show under the veil of dark blue water.

We experienced the nature of Bernheim Forest and went to a Native Dance Pow-Pow at the Cincinnati Zoo, where I heard Native speakers tell their hard-to-swallow history of oppression. I remember the story of the crow whom a boy tied to a car and dragged through the streets for no reason at all outside of excitement.

The Native dancers were so beautiful, and the shingle dresses' sounds were like trickling rain as they danced to heal the world. I read that the shingle-dressed Native women continued to dance during the COVID-19 pandemic to continue to heal the world and the earth of all the damage we continue to do to it.

At the end of the exhibition, we bought a poster, and I went around having the Native dancers, speakers, and all the cute long-haired Native boys sign it.

For Christmas, she took me to the ballet to see the 'Nutcracker'. My mom curled up my hair and dressed me up like a little Victorian porcelain doll. Later, I heard there were times that I dozed off, because the performance was rather long for someone so young, and we had to leave very early to get there, but I don't remember sleeping.

I only recalled the lights, sounds, and costumes. My favorites were the dancers from Clara's dream sequence from all over the world and the wind-up doll ballerina. In recreating this memory, my husband took me to see the Russian Ballet's version of the 'Nutcracker' when they performed at Centre College.

When I taught the Shorris' Study 'A Weapon in the Hands of the Restless Poor', I remembered the experiences I had with Grams and the opportunities she made available. Earl Shorris, in his study, was testing the isolating forces that surround the poor that keep them stuck in their situation.

He argues that people need to engage in the political/global world in order to change their station, the philosophical political world, not just voting, election, and so forth.

Ms. Walker argued that Shorris needs to start earlier, with the children, and show them, *the moral life of downtown*, something Shorris paraphrased as a *moral alternative to the street*. Those plays, movies, and ballets were that alternative, giving the ability to think, reflect, and feel. And Grams gave me that.

My Favorite Doll and The Television

Not long after my mom left, her mother, my Mimi, died. I clearly remember coming into the house, standing at the bay window overlooking the grassy field and the crawdad stream, and my dad pushing the play button on the answering machine. Based on the blooming of the daffodils, it must have been around Easter.

Someone in my mom's family, one of her numerous siblings, left a message about my Mimi's death. My mom was the youngest of 12 children. I don't know my mom's side of the family well.

Actually, it wasn't until my dad showed me my grandmother's headstone, at his new church where he married his third wife, that I realized Mimi's name was Anna Lorean.

I don't have many memories of my Mimi, except the one at the hospital before she died with *the tubes in her wrists*, and one sitting on her couch. She was showing me this tiny book where you hold mirrors to the picture and the mirror finishes the picture. I don't remember many things with her, but I remember feeling loved around her.

My most vivid memory is her funeral which is why I wrote that poem in college, 'My Favorite Doll'. After her funeral, the whole family came into Mimi's home and carried out boxes.

It reminded me of those estate auctions my dad enjoyed going to where they would put numbers on boxes and people would bid, sometimes switching items before bidding started.

It was a weird practice, I remember thinking, watching people eager to take Mimi's stuff. I mean, I get that she couldn't take it with her, but there was something blasphemous about it, intrusive.

As explained in the poem, I was given this doll during the deconstruction of my grandmother's home. It was a very old-fashioned ragdoll with blue plaid patches and strawberries printed across it. I became rather attached to this doll.

Psychologically, it makes perfect sense for a child at five whose mother left and whose grandmother just died to cling to something physical as a sense of comfort. It makes perfect sense I continue to repeat in my brain as an adult when I consider what happened next.

I toted that doll everywhere, and my aunt Sissy went off on tangents about how nasty and old the doll was, complaining about the mildew I'm breathing in. My dad would just laugh and let it go, saying he couldn't get my doll from me if he tried.

When I was toting my doll around the yard at my grandparents' farm while playing with my cousins, one cousin, Sissy's son, ran out the door and took the doll by the feet, and pulled her from my arms. I screamed and held on tight. He ripped her from me, and I was left holding the full front of the doll fabric from the crotch to the neck.

Blue fuzz covered the ground while I cried and others laughed, including the adults. My dad consoled me, explaining she was getting torn up and it was only a matter of time. We had been stitching her piece by piece lately, but this particular tear was too bad to repair because too much of the fabric was shredded.

We ended up putting her body in a little shirt box that I still call her coffin. My aunt laughed and laughed and said her son did me a favor, making me throw out a piece of garbage.

I retold this story to my family by accident one day, as we were playing Carcassonne and listening to my Spotify playlist.

One of my favorite Aerosmith songs came on, 'Rag Doll', so I went into this story, explaining that I was a little too young to understand the story Steven Tyler was singing but I loved the bluesy feel to it and the popping use of Joey Kramer's percussion instruments that did not focus on just drumming. For me the song became about this doll I lost all those years ago.

I found myself sobbing, "Why did they not stop him? Why didn't they understand I needed the doll for a little bit just to hold, just to hang on to? I just lost my mom. My grandmother just died. Why wasn't anyone there protecting me? I was five years old."

Then, embarrassed, I apologized, knowing this wasn't the time or place, but everyone was fine. It led to a different discussion with my husband and daughter, about how memories trigger and when authority figures shouldn't have so much power.

After my mom left, my grandmother died, and a cousin, encouraged by his mother, savagely ripped up my doll, my favorite television show, 'She-Ra', was canceled and no one thought to tape the Christmas special for me.

I graduated from kindergarten that year.

My dad had been working construction for a bit, but just got a job at the Toyota Plant. His hours included a lot of overtime, and he had a long commute to Georgetown from ours.

Bardstown home. Needless to say, he was not at my graduation, but he invited Sissy and Pam to fill in for him.

My mom was beautiful. She had on slick red lipstick and what looked like a little business suit with a pencil skirt. I ran to her and showed her what the school gave me, a red carnation and a sketch of my silhouette done with black paper glued to pink cardstock.

As I handed her these gifts, Sissy reached out and took them from me, saying, "Oh, Honey, look at the things for *your dad*," getting into a tug of war with my mom who had the picture already in her hand.

In a hushed voice, the one my mom uses when correcting us publicly, she said, "My daughter is giving these to me."

Sissy replies, "Honey, these are for your dad. You want to give these to your dad, don't you?"

It didn't sound like a question, more like a command, and I was clearly pulled in the middle. The rest of the graduation was a watery blur. I am not sure if I ever got the red carnation to my mom or not.

I remember the teacher though, and the look of pity in her eyes, a look of pity I have seen throughout my life by numerous teachers at their realization of what is happening in my life. The look of *Oh, she doesn't have a mother. She just has a dad, and he doesn't know any better.*

The notes were sent home requesting the parents' help tying shoes or needing proper clothes, so their kid will no longer break the dress code due to growing or needing proper food in the lunchbox for field trips. That constant look of a *poor child raised by a dumb man* got old.

It was around third grade when my dad decided he needed to live closer to work so he could spend adequate time at home for sleep and family. He ended up renting a place in Frankfort while a house was being built in Georgetown. It was not a great area to live. They were duplexes on the border of Frankfort and Georgetown.

My dad would get home very late, oftentimes bringing home fast food for dinner. I remember being the kind of kid who hated it when the teachers brought candy as treats. Honestly, I would prefer if someone would bring in sandwiches. My dad, bless his heart, tried, but he could not seem to work a stove.

When he'd make kids' cuisine, the corn or vegetable section was still frozen or coated in ice and the main entree was burned. When he made fried bologna, he cut an X in the center instead of around the sides. However, I do have fond memories of when we'd have the frozen meal with the slices of turkey in a gravy.

It made me wonder how someone, as hardworking as he was, who lived on a farm with nine other brothers and sisters couldn't seem to make a meal and relied so heavily on frozen meals which is not as cost-effective as knowing how to cook, at least not for a family.

Once when my husband and I were grocery shopping and he suggested the penguin-themed dinosaur nugget kids cuisine, he got an earful of what I thought about meals like that. They're unnecessary expenses for barely any food, and how I could cook just fine. It took a while for me to unpack the anger directed at a frozen dinner. Turns out, I was simply used to food deserts and gas station meals.

I don't remember the elementary school in Frankfort very well, just that I was sleeping a lot. The whole memory is like a sleepy haze. At times, teachers would leave me in the wrong room when I fell asleep. I would wake up in the music room or the book fair and have to track down the teacher.

It was years later that I realized this was my punishment. At the time, I was just sad I had been forgotten and upset that the teachers would just abandon me in a part of a building I was unfamiliar with, not realizing that *was* the intention.

At least at the time, I realized I was not responsible for the sleepy haze that I walked in throughout the day. As a teacher now myself, I am upset these teachers did not realize there was a bigger picture to see.

At this time, my third-grade brain truly thought teachers became teachers because they hated children and enjoyed tormenting them. This was confirmed this year at Hern Elementary when I was trick-or-treating and found a teacher's house.

She was giving out candy I hated because it hurt my teeth, the peanut butter taffy candy wrapped in black and orange. As an educator now, situations like this come to mind sporadically and make me wonder if my behavior makes students feel this way too.

I remember shocking that same teacher when I told her I would be moving in with my mother soon, as my mother continued to tell us. The teacher jumped up in shock. Her abrupt movement and shock made me think I was in trouble, so I cried.

She took me to a counseling group that met weekly about divorce. While it did get the sleeping child out of the classroom, it did very little good, except introduce me to the idea that some kids blame themselves for their parents' divorce, a thought that never occurred to me.

I remember the soft whispering voice of the teacher, or most likely a counselor, saying to our group, "I need you all to know that you did not cause your parents to divorce."

I almost laughed, but well…I was sleepy. The thought of being the cause of the divorce *never* crossed my mind. I often blamed my dad for throwing my mom on the lawn all those years ago. I've heard hushed rumors about my mom having boyfriends, lots of them, and multiple affairs.

Since my dad's second wife supposedly had an affair and my sister *ran away*, I don't carry much stock in the fiction my dad likes to weave around his circumstances. Hell, I've seen him brag about a fictitious account of my life on Facebook.

But the big reason my parents got a divorce is because they were children who had no business getting married, so I *never* blamed myself.

When in Frankfort, the relationships between my sisters and dad were changing. Summer was growing up and getting a little sick of being the woman of the house, responsible for everything, and he just moved her away from her family and friends.

I am not sure exactly what happened, but I know my dad's rage and I know Summer, who had the responsibility of a parent, had started a relationship. Since my dad was not home until late, Summer had free range of her life as an adult, and I guess my dad did not like what he came home to one day. Summer was found in her room with a boy.

The story I heard was always that my sister ran away from home because my dad called the police on her. Summer tells a different story, which was corroborated by a cut on her face from being hit and cutting her lip on her braces. She said he tossed her outside with her clothes shoved in trash bags. My dad willingly relinquished custody of Summer.

Then, he started sending her over-the-top gifts with letters. One gift was a beautiful emerald ring he got at an estate sale. The stone was large, and the setting was elaborately ornate and included rows of diamonds in a spiral around the side.

Summer sent it back, *returned it to the sender*, and explained to him in written form that his gifts are forms of manipulation.

Later that year, my dad was sent to Japan for three months for training, so had to move back to Bardstown with my aunt Sissy. She was a weird stay-at-mom like the young babysitter who isn't much older than the children being babysat, and she seems to hate the children she is responsible for, even if two of which are her own.

She would accuse us of stealing from my dad when we needed something. I had this bird, and when I would clean its cage, I put down little sandpaper liners. For example, when I asked if I could have more, my aunt yelled that I had my own money and shouldn't be stealing from my dad like that.

When I talked to my dad later on the phone, instead of understanding that I was hurt for being accused of stealing things he used to buy for me, he praised my aunt for the suggestion and told me to start paying for supplies for my pets myself.

The best thing about living with my aunt was my two cousins had the coolest toys. I was the youngest of three, so I was pretty comfortable with hand-me-downs, but her kids had all the latest toys: the big pillow window guy DJ from Full House had, mountains of my little ponies, My Pet Monster with the orange plastic chains on her little fluffy wrists, viewfinders, Light Brites, and glow worms and Popples. I loved Popples.

They were bright and fuzzy little critters that had a slip of material that could make a pouch. The pouch would extend around the critter to turn it into a furry little ball like when Sonic spins collecting rings. Sissy's kids had the white Popple, Puffball.

That's not to say I didn't have my whole Looney Tune wallpapered toy box tube. I would spend my days crawling inside and playing in my own basement, but we didn't live there anymore. We were make shifting between multiple housing environments until our house was built.

But the worst thing about living with my aunt was she would also start yelling during after-school cartoons if we were loud another day while she was watching her stories. It was weird, and I loved my TV, especially my afternoon cartoons.

I vividly recall the feeling in my chest, that Christmas morning pang of my heart, when I would hear the chime of the block letter word Filmation being spelled across the screen prior to She-Ra's theme song. The television was important to me. It had always been there to greet me. It passed the time with me.

It had consistently been there with some familiar voices or, for cartoons at the time, a lesson. Mildred's life in 'Fahrenheit 451' reminded me of my life, days filled with relatives projected on screens and their non-descriptive incomprehensible lives were a comfort to me, like someone sitting in the empty room with me.

The television was the white noise that filled my day, so when Sissy was interrupting my cartoons, I really just wanted her to Shut. The. Fuck. Up.

Ode to my Television: A love story

We all act on impulse
and emotion,
Every action is a coping mechanism,
In an attempt to preserve.

I remember the constant in my life.
The television
It was always there waiting for me,
Like some latchkey kid, reeking of loneliness,
Too young to go out,

A house too empty for company
Like the pathetic wife in *Fahrenheit*
With the television wall filled with *relatives*
It had little to do with the plot,
It was just to have someone there.
To stave off the loneliness.

So, my life was filled with Sam,
Melons Ross Gears, and Frasier Cranes
Rose Nilane

I find myself as an adult turning on my streaming service
And walking away
Watching nothing
But just having someone else in the room,

Someone familiar.

The Evil Queen and the Red-Headed Stepchild

I was 10 years old when my dad married Number Two not long after Autumn moved out.

My husband says I place a lot of my bad memories and hateful feelings toward this woman because it makes it easier to love my dad. I hate this woman to the very core of my soul. I hate her bitchy little face, her little yappy dog, and the dog's little seat on the armrest. But I didn't always feel this way. It was hard alone with my dad without my sisters.

He was hateful and disinterested. He seemed to be angry he had to parent at all, and he was clearly on the market to outsource these responsibilities.

When I was sick and about eye level with the cabinets under the sink in the kitchen so about four or five, my dad tried to give me cold medicine in the middle of the night while my sisters slept. The pill was large and clearly not children's medication nor was it chewable, and I struggled with swallowing pills.

Ironically, I still do. My throat seems to lock up while I'm swallowing and once it slides down my throat, it may come back up like a strange gag reflex. The pill came back up slightly dissolved.

He was so upset he pulled me by my arm and slammed me multiple times face-first into the cabinet. He wasn't the type of parent who would take care of sick kids. He never saw it as his job.

Just like when the teachers would send home homework, he'd get so upset when they would request parents' help or the audacity of asking him to read with me which was a waste of his time.

Even though due to our moves, there were clearly educational gaps that could not be entirely addressed in the classroom. Why on Earth would highly qualified teachers request untrained overworked parents to help them with work? For the love of God, teachers, stop asking parents to help their children!

When I could not process the math problem quickly, he would hit me on the top of my head with the bottom of his fist. It wasn't surprising I was bad at math. When I was in elementary school, I would cry at number recall tests because I could not process the number when I heard the word.

I didn't understand how the word 40 translates to the numbers 4 and 0 together. My dad was more of a numbers guy, so he did not sympathize that I couldn't see them in my mind the way he did. I was never a math person, and there was a certain bit of trauma related to it.

Once, after a parent contact by my fifth-grade teacher, my dad went through my backpack and found my read-along extra credit handout to be filled out by parents wadded up in my backpack, so he yelled at me, demanding a title to write on the handout. I explained that the assignment was not required, and it was for a read-along with a parent.

He yelled again, "What book?" his voice seemed to shake the wall.

I quickly said, "The Babysitter's Club, but it is a read-along with the parent."

He sneered, "It is not my job to do your work."

I was so embarrassed. Not only did I lie, but I had to bring this sheet to the pull-out reading class I was placed in filled with all these bad kids from classes who were really mean. No one had done these handouts, and they laughed when I turned in my sheet.

The teacher had this cutesy reinforcement chart and placed a star next to my name. At the end of the month, for being in the lead on the chart, I was rewarded with a carousel pencil that I quickly gave to a younger student.

When I was praised, he was worse because he'd try to claim the validation for himself. In fourth grade, the state of Kentucky started writing portfolios. My teacher was so impressed with my work of fiction about climbing up my bunk bed which turned into a treehouse-like portal into another world, and my toys and I would go on adventures.

Honestly, I was simply scripting some of my pretend play, and I really enjoyed it. After a parent-teacher conference, my dad came home and asked to see the story which he rewrote entirely, ruining my writing voice, distorting what I was saying, and making it his own. I felt so bad that I removed the story from my portfolio, and I was incredibly angry with my teacher.

The teachers need to realize that sometimes communication with parents is the worst thing for the child, something I still struggle with as a teacher. I often joke that the worst part of my job is not the numerous papers to grade or behavior management, but rather the parent contacts.

I never know what situation I am walking into. I don't know if a child is in a safe environment or not. I don't know if my piddly request for missing work is met with abuse or love.

I did get revenge though. These homework sessions with my dad were brutal. When working on writing assignments, my dad would always require me to look up words he or I didn't know how to spell in the dictionary. When reading over something I wrote, he said I needed to look up the word *cannot*.

I said, "Why? What's wrong with it?"

He said, "It is misspelled."

"It's not."

"Yes, it is. You gave it two Ns. Look it up," he said and shoved the dictionary toward me.

I shoved it back and replied, "If you don't know how to spell it, you look it up. I know how to spell *cannot*."

He smugly looked up the word, turned red, and glared at me. As I said, he was more of a numbers guy and maybe, there was a reason he hated it when teachers asked him to read to me; which he never did. Maybe he struggled with reading.

At least, when my mom left and couldn't read to me, she gave me fairy tale books with a cassette tape that would read a page and chime when the page was turned. I loved listening to 'Rumpelstiltskin' and 'The Emperor's New Clothes'. There was a book on each side of the cassette.

Number Two lived in Frankfort and worked as a legal secretary. They met at square dancing. Like my dad, she was a single parent. She had a round chubby face with soft facial features, framed with kinky curls cut short. She had a slight hint of rosacea and was incredibly uncomfortable with her very slight weight issue.

I remember her being very kind until she moved in. She went through my dad's buffet, emptied it of my papers, markers, and letters, and told me to put my crap away. She took down my dad's 8x10 framed pictures of each of us that hung above the large living room window and hung curtains, but then never re-hung the school pictures.

In the hallway toward their bedroom, she hung a very beautiful picture from her senior year of herself standing next to a tree with her hair styled like Princess Diana, razored at her neck. I remember this photo very well.

I was quite scandalized by the photo at that time, having never seen a woman style their hair in this way, because I thought she looked weird and boyish. My mom had taught me girls don't cut their hair, so my hair was always crazy long and slightly unkempt, 'The Clan of the Cave Bear'.

I knew Number Two was not the person to braid my hair. I found the lack of family pictures replaced by her senior picture very vain.

The year after they were married, she immediately bought a huge Douglas Fir Christmas tree when they went on sale after Christmas. She went and bought up the huge garish purple and gold ball and spiral ornaments for these storefront-style Christmas trees. I hated it. She took all my ornaments, including the photo ball ornament with a woven thread backing, reading 1982, in a box at the end of the stairs.

The ball ornament was my first Christmas and included the photo of the three of us with Summer holding me as a baby. Before I got home, the box of ornaments, ones I made as a kid, got moved off the steps and placed in the garage next to the trash can, the clothespin reindeer, and the felt mouse. I was furious, but I did end up giving those ornaments to my mother for her tree.

Since Number Two stole the joy out of putting up a Christmas tree, I got my own small tree and took all the special ornaments Grams got me each year and hung them myself. I had the greatest tree, strung with memories.

They might not match, but they bring me joy as I would unwrap those memories like little gifts like the tiny glass ballerina representing the little tease about standing on my tippy toes and Clara's bed surrounded by all the characters from the Nutcracker that when plugged into a Christmas light would spin as though in a dance.

The purple and gold monstrosity was a two-day ordeal that no one helped with and required the use of a ladder. Once, Number Two started a business and opened her store, Christmas got really chaotic, so the garish tree was put up twice.

She came up with weird rules too. After school, I wasn't allowed to open the door even though I regularly played outside before my dad got home from work. She expected me to rudely leave my friends waiting on the porch and let them knock and knock. Friends, with whom I would play basketball down the street until the street lights came on.

Friends who I ate dinner with sometimes. Friends who I climbed trees with and explored areas too dangerous to admit to exploring. Friends who I climbed fences with and walked on the property of God knows who.

Friends who walked to Speedway with me around the highway. *Don't open the door?* Spare me!

You cannot treat a child like they can manage themselves and then expect them to follow obnoxious rules that do not apply to them.

She was furious when I opened the door to let my friends know I wasn't allowed to play until someone got home. Rolling our eyes, my friends and I moved on, but then she came home earlier screaming about safety, blah, blah, blah. My dad explained that she came from a bad part of town, and I just needed to let her have this one.

Once she started a chore chart that she read about in a co-parenting book. I didn't mind taking turns cleaning the bathroom once a week and vacuuming the stairs. It was reasonable to ask us to do chores, but what made it odd was it was not for two children but four people total.

I looked at her like she was a Martian, and said, "You think you are going to assign my dad chores? That's not going to work out well."

She glared at me and said, "He does stuff around the house."

"I know. But you should not be assigning him chores. This is not going to go well."

I tried to warn her, but she didn't listen and the chore chart, except our upstairs rotation of cleaning the bathroom and vacuuming the stairs, disappeared entirely.

As soon as she moved in, I immediately got in trouble for not owning a bathrobe which was weird because I was 10 years old and wasn't in charge of purchasing my clothing yet, nor would I ever consider needing a robe when a towel is functional.

When I walked out of the bathroom after my shower and took the 10 steps to my bedroom door, she started screaming, "You are not to walk around like that with my son in the house."

I had always lived with women and never considered my body in a towel to be an issue. Why was she sexualizing a 10-year-old girl's body in her own home? That week, we had to get a bathrobe.

I don't fully understand why she made such a big deal considering I was 10 holding a towel, but when John's friend spent the night, snuck under my bed after my shower, and looked at my body in my full-length mirror as I got dressed, I was to be quiet about it and not tell my dad, so John did not lose privileges.

Like my dad, Number Two would fly into unreasonable rage often. One of the most unreasonable fits of rage she had, other than a bathrobe, was about menstruation. Since John and I switched cleaning the bathroom weekly, I always made sure that my pads were folded up and wrapped heavily with toilet paper. However, this was not good enough.

She marched me into the bathroom where John stood, wiping down the mirror, opened the trash can, and yelled at me, "How do you think this makes him feel?"

After that, I was no longer allowed to dispose of my feminine hygiene products in the shared bathroom. It was ridiculously stupid and made me more and more ashamed of my body.

Building on creating more body image issues, she would make little comments about my body like how the high arches on mine and my dad's feet made us look deformed, or when she asked my doctor treating my scoliosis if my large breasts were a problem.

To this day, I still appreciate the look of disgust on his face when answering her ridiculous question with, "They'd have to be abnormally big to hurt her back. She's fine."

I could not help it if she wasn't the fairest of all, and I looked too much like my mother for a woman, so uncomfortable with herself.

She would glare at me when my dad would tell me I was pretty in my black suspender pants and white shirt and I'd respond, "I know it."

Honestly, we should all feel that way about ourselves, but she tried hard to chip that confidence away, that confidence she did not possess about herself.

I'm not certain why they got married at all. I remember listening to this woman explain to a friend: how everything seemed to fall into place, how she met this guy who had a three-bedroom house, one-bedroom was open for John because Autumn had moved out.

Had Autumn still lived here, she would have chased her away, how they had some high phone bills due to talking to each other while they dated, and how when she wrecked her car, he provided one. Basically, the gist of her conversation was that, financially, things fell into place.

She saw all this as a sign that everything was meant to be instead, he just purchased her and needed another woman to run the household now that Autumn wasn't there to keep everything in order. My dad was pretty helpless when it came to basic life skills. He worked like an ox but was about as bright.

They fought all the time. Once during a family trip to Pigeon Forge, their fight started during the road trip and continued until we got to the hotel. It was our first family trip, a *bonding experience*. After we got through the door of the hotel, Number Two went for a drive where she would speed around dangerously.

When she left, she mentioned something about hoping to wrap the car around a pole. Eventually, things calmed down, and we played a family game of Trivial Pursuit which isn't the best family game for a variety of ages, and honestly, my dad is infamous for being a very poor support and cheating.

He'd argue that in Monopoly you had to pay attention, or else he had the right to skip turns, steal money, and miss doubles on dice; and when teaching me checkers in the dentist's office, he cheated when I started winning by calling moves a forced move and would force my pieces away from the sides so he could jump them easily.

Once when playing putt-putt, he had been doing so poorly on a hole that he made us restart and take turns after each putt like croquet instead of having us finish our full turn. He turned a 6+ putt into a birdie. However, Trivial Pursuit was fun for a bit until we hit some seriously hard and boring categories.

Number Two suggested modifying the rules to continue to have fun, but my dad argued that we follow the rules, or we don't play, saying something derogatory about her level of knowledge, implying she was too stupid to play properly, even though no one was having fun anymore.

I once asked my dad, after a very loud argument, when he came to tuck me in, "Why did you marry her?"

Clearly, he came to tuck me in to get away from her a little bit, so he didn't mind this type of discussion with me.

He replied, "Because it was convenient."

One of their major arguments was financial. I remember watching Number Two cry when my cat dug up the plants she was placing in the planter.

She mumbled to herself, "I'm not allowed to have anything."

My dad had come home after an estate sale and bought a framed print of a violin with gold foil on the print. It was a pricey purchase for him, but kind of a hobby as well. Number Two started yelling at him, especially considering how he lectured her about how much she spent on groceries.

He told her that if she contributed more to the overall household expenses, she'd have more of a say over their finances. I don't think any amount she spent on groceries would be sufficient to him, because it was never about the total but the fact that she was making a financial decision.

Meals would include a diatribe by Number Two, explaining the cost of everything she purchased, how much she saved, and what the meal cost per person. He'd mostly ignore her.

Clearly, the convenience was that he had open rooms in the house they could occupy which gave him a way to take her paycheck. I felt sorry for her. It wasn't right to just take her money and act like he was doing her a favor.

One year for Christmas, he gave her a tennis bracelet that she would gush over, making her forget that she had no financial control, and he could make a decision with their money like it was an extravagant gift, and she graciously thanked him. Her bracelet reminded me of Summer's emerald ring, a manipulation.

When they were first married, they did a lot of things together. They continued to square dance and started camping. Number Two really wanted a camper and desired to camp regularly. She was very sociable too and had a friend with children John's age, but slowly, these activities stopped.

They became less and less important, and the poor lady became more and more isolated. Maybe that was my dad's intention. No friend would allow another woman to be treated this way and the treatment toward her slowly got worse, to the point that maybe, it was less noticeable.

Once, when Number Two was running late after work because she was still commuting from Frankfort, she asked my dad to make dinner. He was so mad about it that he excluded her son John from the dinner table. He heated up a couple of hot dogs, saying John had already eaten because two hot dogs were missing.

After lots of yelling, they decided to put in place rules about after-school snacks and what specifically constitutes a snack, and what constitutes a meal. Unfortunately, that means cereal was no longer a snack. Since they didn't really buy snacks, we no longer ate after school before dinner at all.

His treatment of John was the most problematic, one that I kind of judge Number Two for allowing for so long and staying in a marriage while her child endured such poor treatment. John was a chubby little boy with orange freckles across the bridge of his nose and curly red hair that Brillos out if he let it grow too long. He was quite literally the red-headed stepchild.

I am fortunate because my husband adopted my son when he turned seven, and his whole family rallied around him as he became their first grandchild. Biological or not, they love my son dearly as their own because he was.

However, when he introduced his new family members to co-workers at Kings Island on Toyota day he did so as, "My wife and her son."

Not stepson. Her son. Distancing himself.

He continued to distance himself from John, which got worse as John got older. He'd yell about the sound of John's footsteps in the house. When there was a plumbing issue, instead of looking into it, he accused John of using too much toilet paper.

When moving in, he expected a 12-year-old boy to put his furniture in a second floor bedroom and fill up his own waterbed with no help at all. My dad, maybe due to his own upbringing, thinks boys are full-grown independent adults, and women are children who need to be provided for and governed.

When I think about my dad's treatment of John, I often think about my dad and his relationship with my Pepaw. While my Pepaw was a decent enough man, his emphasis on education was at times used as a dig to some of his children, like my dad who did not cut it in college.

My grandfather had dropped out of school in sixth grade and could barely read. He would tell stories about how he'd have to memorize the order of the letters on boxes at the warehouse when sorting because he could not read the labels.

While he encouraged the importance of education, he would still ask why there was an N— on the cover of my copy of 'Uncle Tom's Cabin'. Not everything he said was valuable. Validation and some kind words from my Pepaw would have done my dad a world of good which brings to mind the time my dad won a Camry for perfect attendance.

Attendance was really important to my dad, so much so that we were not allowed to get sick. When I was denied my half dollar at the end of the year school awards, my dad called the elementary school and demanded to know why.

He was furious to discover that his brother who picked me up once bypassed the pickup line and took me out of school five minutes earlier, impacting my perfect attendance record.

He also got upset with my mom who refused to send Autumn to school with a 102° temperature. He would often medicate us before school if we were running a fever or throwing up. Tums or cold medicine could be found in my backpack often.

While raising children as a single parent, having long commutes before moving closer to the plant, and going to custody battles multiple times; winning a car for perfect attendance was truly an accomplishment, one that he had every right to be proud of, but his dad wasn't hearing it.

Instead of being impressed by a free car, he chastised my dad again for working for Japs and thinking he got a free car. My Pepaw explained that Toyota did not give my dad a car; they gave him a bill because he had to claim the car as income and pay the taxes on it.

My dad protested, explaining that Toyota also covered those expenses, and these were part of his benefits, but Pepaw heard nothing. My dad was silent the whole way home, embarrassed and ashamed, so it isn't all that surprising that my dad was so resentful of John, but that did not excuse the behavior either.

When he realized that two additional people in the house cost more, he forced Number Two to sue her ex-husband for child support which she never got. It angered my dad because he had to provide for someone else's kid which he often mentioned.

John never saw his dad after the request for child support until he was an adult, completely estranging himself from his father.

With no father, my dad had a perfect opportunity to step into John's life. He didn't have sons of his own and could have been a father figure, if not a father just a positive male role model.

Instead, he was so incredibly upset at his existence that John was made to feel like an intruder who shit too large and stepped too heavily in his house. John ended up getting a job and rarely coming home.

Number Two would compensate for my dad's poor treatment of John by taking it out on his daughters and his family. She stopped visiting my dad's very large extended family. He was the oldest boy of 10 children. While she was polite enough, she would complain about her headache on the way home, because a large southern family can be loud and boisterous.

She would complain about how they would all talk over each other, and she could not seem to follow one conversation.

Then, she started getting really nasty, explaining to my dad how she was from a different type of family than he was and how funny it would be if she was riding with her Disneyland dad or grandmother and passed all these rednecks hanging off a truck like the Clampetts, never considering that there was her future husband.

In a southern family, there is a playfulness and a meanness that are intended as bonding. Unfortunately, my dad and his siblings did this very poorly because they picked at things that were real and hurt people.

In an action, intended to welcome her into the family, Bobby, my uncle, walked up to her and said, "Every time I see you, you always eat."

Number Two had a noticeable weight problem, one that she was very sensitive about, which was exacerbated by her inability to select appropriate foods due to their cost and being surrounded by my dad's beautiful daughters.

Bobby went to jail for owning property where marijuana was growing. Number Two carried the pain of a careless comment throughout the whole time he was in prison and was eager to see him when he got out because she had lost so much weight.

It wasn't like he called her deformed, threatened to take her child, or yelled at her for menstruating, so I'm not sure what her beef was.

With Autumn, she complained about everything Autumn had, like she was in competition, especially once they opened the collectible store. She fantasized about opening a museum, requiring that she own one of each item from her collectible store.

Autumn had collected Noah's Ark things and whenever she picked out things she liked, Number Two needed to keep those same items for herself.

My dad and Number Two helped Autumn open a franchise-type store in another town, so they could sell through the secondary market at an elevated price that was not allowed by a typical retail brick-and-mortar store with certain wholesale accounts.

She took account of everything Autumn purchased to ensure she did not have more, and she was furious when Autumn was successful, so much so, that after Autumn became a nurse, she pursued a nursing degree too.

When Autumn got married, Number Two said, "I hope Russel doesn't convince her to have children with him. Then, she'd never get rid of him," because clearly anything Autumn had, including her own marriage, needed to fail before this Evil Queen would be happy.

While she was jealous of Autumn, she hated Summer, probably due to Summer's loving spirit and kind heart. She constantly talked about Summer like she was white trash.

While she loved watching Summer's two children, she would make comments about how Summer was constantly looking for child care and financial help which was odd because Summer wouldn't allow people to do too much for her, because she found out earlier the cost of someone's help.

She knew gifts were manipulation and help came with strings. That is why she paid for her own wedding. She had a lot of pride and a good heart, which is what the Evil Queen wanted locked in a box in the first place.

My dad and Number Two bought Summer's kids clothes only during their visits but the clothes were never sent home. She would complain about the kids' clothes, how they were always hand-me-downs, or ill-fitting clothes bought at the wrong size off of clearance racks.

You'd think that a woman who cried when she couldn't pay for her meal when she went Dutch on dates with my dad would understand the necessity of living within your means and making do.

And then, there was me. There were plenty of other things that clearly communicated, "I don't want you around."

Once, after hanging out with my boyfriend on a school night, I got chastised for being home early. My curfew was 9 pm but I got home at 7 pm, so I could finish my homework, and honestly, teenage hormones do not need the additional temptation of endless time with one another.

Number Two taunted, "What are you doing home this early? This is enough time for him to pick up another date for the evening."

I had homework, but it turns out I found that I could do my homework and everything else I needed to at my boyfriend's house because clearly, the expectation was I was not to be home every school day until 9 pm; weekends were later.

But that is what was communicated to me, "Don't be here."

I guess it made sense. They didn't have to feed me. They didn't need to know where I was, nor were they all that concerned. It was odd to me to realize other friends did not have that kind of freedom.

They couldn't just jump in the car and see where the wind was taking us because they needed to know where we were going, how long we'd be there when they'd be home, and if/when they ate dinner. Things concerned parents do. Make sure they know where their kid is and whether they have eaten or not.

The downside was it created a weird almost cohabitation situation with me and the boyfriend, making the relationship more serious than necessary. I started fading into his family. We would attend family holidays together.

There were always gifts for me from his family under their tree and visa-versa. It is sad looking back at it all. Teenage relationships end. Nothing against the young boy I tied to all my dreams, but we just weren't going in the same direction in life, and it was challenging ending our relationship that it became almost a shacking-up situation.

I did not handle the end of the relationship well, especially as it got more and more controlling. I tried often to break up with him, and he'd just tell me no or he'd show up. It got a little scary at times.

I ended up immediately getting into a sexual relationship with someone else quickly, a relationship destined to fail, but this sexual relationship also resulted in a pregnancy.

Instead of supporting me through the challenging time of that relationship ending, my dad simply said, "You need to show more appreciation for his mother. She did a lot for you. She has been there for you often."

Huh, yeah Dad, because you weren't. And now, I'm ungrateful. Again. Always ungrateful for not allowing other people to decide my life. Always ungrateful. If it costs so much for people to do things for me, maybe everyone should stop if it comes with all these strings of obedience. Fuck that!

Then, to add insult to injury, Number Two tells my ex-boyfriend, "You deserved better," which he told me as well as every mutual friend we had.

Clearly, this painting of me in everyone's brain needed to be monstrous.

I'm not sure what kind of life Number Two dreamed of, but it wasn't ever an attainable thing. Maybe she wanted the white picket fence and everything that the image represented which manifested as family trips, furniture, curtains, paint/wallpaper, plants, and a garish Macy's tree.

Maybe that is what she meant by *meant to be*. She needed a way out of her poverty, and my dad offered that ladder, but like with everything, there is a string on that ladder, and it can work like a bungee cord.

She did not become an evil queen, a Mother Gothel, until she stayed in the marriage too long, like in 'Lord of the Flies', how they become more savage the longer they were on the island. She was very much the character Roger with the stick sharpened at both ends, typical behavior for a wounded animal.

Evil Queen

She repainted the hallway,
Mauve,
Half wallpapered,
In shell patterns,
Invades.

She broke through the doorway,
A week before I left,
Seals my life with duct tape.

Summers spent in an overnight-bag,
In her doll display room
On a borrowed bed.

Square Peg in a Round Hole

When I was pregnant with my first child, I was 21 years old. Unmarried. And in a bind. My dad told me to come home, and he'd help. His help consisted of putting me on government assistance and taking it from me to pay my car insurance. With the food stamps, they would buy stuff for their lunches for work.

I vividly remember the 20 oz. bottles of Pepsi that lined the fridge and the jubilant attitude my dad had about that free money that I didn't need because they were being so generous. Gratitude has such a cost, and I remember feeling it in the pit of my stomach.

The yellow wallpaper was so confining, and this madwoman was so eager to peel it away. I lived off blocks of WIC cheese and cereal. Sometimes, if the money didn't run out after paying my car insurance, I would scrape together three dollars to buy a protein-based meal at Burger King which included a simple burger, fries, and a coke. It tasted magical.

I also started looking in the pantry for food they would not notice missing. Typically, the food was the crumbs at the bottom of the bag of chips or a smooshy banana. I'll never forget the taste of the stale, unfortunately, lime-flavored chips. I gagged and threw up.

At times, my dad and Number Two would invite me to dinner when they would go to a restaurant. They went daily, but I was not always invited. I remember going to Olive Garden for lunch. It was an odd lunch choice because their prices did not change for lunch. They had one main menu.

When I ordered, my dad turned to me and said, "You think you are worth that? You think you did anything today to get something like that."

He also berated the waitress for the lack of a lunch menu and the prices of the food. I wanted to crawl under the table. At the time, I was getting noticeably pregnant, and it was clear he hated the very sight of me.

However, their scenes at restaurants were pretty typical like a routine or better yet a charade. They would nit-pick, get a server flustered, call a manager, and see how much they could get for free. It was a big game to them which probably cost people their jobs.

They would brag about how for two consecutive years on their anniversary they were getting a free meal at Ruby Tuesdays because of poor service and the importance of the occasion. Years later, Ruby Tuesdays at that same location closed, and to this day, I still blame them.

Once, they were complaining so much over a manager seating another couple 30 seconds before us accidentally: claiming that the couple had the better server, a better table, quicker drinks, etc., that the man from the table apologized to my dad and offered to switch tables.

I wanted to turn to him and say, "They do this. It gets their meals comped," but decided against it.

When I lived with them, I also had to march to job interviews with the expectation that I was to conceal my pregnancy. I remember leaving for a job interview for a daycare center that I actually attended.

I put on my best maternity clothes that my sister bought me at a consignment store. I thought I looked pretty. The patterns were a little dated and the shirt was long enough to cover the elastic on the navy blue slacks.

My dad sighed exasperated, "Can't you look less pregnant?"

When I got to the interview, I felt stupid and ugly. The conversation with the lady was nice. I was clearly not who they wanted because they would prefer to have someone with childcare courses, but I did have a history of babysitting and had worked in a daycare in high school one summer.

At the end, she looked at me knowingly, and said, "Is there anything you'd like to tell me about yourself?"

I responded no and quickly left, feeling the size of my stomach and the discomfort of the hot southern summer.

Number Two set up a pantry downstairs for my food, so my food was completely separate from theirs, mainly macaroni and cheese and boxes of noodles. She had a weight problem and was a devout follower of 'Weight Watchers'.

Her food was packaged up and labeled with points, so everything in the house was closely calculated. When I would heat up my food and eat, she would stand over me and remind me I'd be fat eating an entire box of mac and cheese for a meal. She did not seem to care that this was my daily meal or maybe, even consider this fact.

After having my son, I had to march to new interviews. Fortunately, due to a snap in my shoulder, I wasn't able to work for Toyota, so I could simply return to school instead of being required to follow in my dad's footsteps and not pursue my dreams. I did end up getting a job at Cracker Barrel while I finished my bachelor's degree.

Due to my new job, I needed new clothes for their uniform: khaki pants and a white button-down shirt with a collar. Number Two agreed to take me to Goodwill to find what I needed, but she left out an important detail.

We did not have much luck finding what I needed but I was told to take what they had anyway: white shirts and a pair of tan colored jeans. I knew I wouldn't be allowed to wear them. It wasn't the uniform, but since she insisted and she agreed to take me, I could not argue.

However, since she was forcing the purchase and offered to take me, I assumed she was paying but when we got to the register, she stood there waiting for me to pay, for clothes that I did not want that would not work for my job. I opened my wallet and unfolded my three dollars. No Burger King today. And still no clothes for work.

I had worked at Barnes and Noble for a while but after the holidays, my hours were drastically cut, so much so that Number Two insisted I had two options: get better hours or quit. Otherwise, she'd come to work and leave my son there.

I was very much a prisoner in their house. When I'd get to their house after work or class, I would bring my son to my room and do my homework, often while giving him his bottle. He was a really quiet baby, so quiet that the doctor told me to wake him up to feed him.

He started sleeping all night after three days. Having to leave my baby with someone was a challenge. He was so tiny, and I was so afraid he wouldn't be returned. Once, I woke up in the middle of the night and didn't see him in my sleepy state. I woke up Number Two, demanding my son, only to be walked back to my room to see him sleeping in the baby bed next to me.

After watching my precious tiny baby, Number Two would go into detail about everything she wasn't able to do because of my son. She made sure I knew daily that she was doing me a huge favor that was a huge inconvenience to her.

However, she was thrilled when he would stay in the swing all day because she'd just leave him there rocking back and forth, even though he hadn't eaten and rarely cried due to hunger as the doctor said.

I would feed him immediately, knowing she didn't. When my dad would get home, he'd demand to see his grandson, so I would bring him downstairs and return to my homework.

Then, he'd yell at me again, saying, "I'm not a babysitter. You stay here and watch your kid," so I'd sit on the floor watching my kid on his boppy watching 'Andy Griffin' instead of my German homework.

Before leaving for work, I would get some playtime with my son but if my dad was there, he would rush me out, saying I was wasting time and needed to leave. It felt like every time I was enjoying anything, he'd yell at me; like being a parent was supposed to be miserable and if there was joy in my life, he needed to take it as a punishment.

Technically, living under their roof, I would not be able to get food stamps because of their combined income.

However, we did try to get on food stamps appropriately and legally, once I lived with them, but when I put my address on the sign-in page, the lady at the office yelled at me in the waiting room.

She told me I did not live in that area; she knew where it was and what it cost and told me to leave. It was humiliating. Since I had a rental apartment for the remainder of the summer where I attended college, I was able to use this address and lack of income to qualify, but once my lease was up, I no longer qualified.

Yes, this is a fraud, but I did not have a choice. Literally, beggars can't be choosers, and I was indeed, a beggar at this point. I still wonder why they went through so much trouble for barely six hundred dollars.

After I did not qualify, my dad's wife, Number Two, tried to write me a *permission slip* explaining the cost of healthy food and her dietary needs which I was to give them when reapplying with their address. I refused. She got heated with me, so I told her to call herself and I'd be more than willing to comply with her demands.

She did not bring it up again, so with a Cheshire cat smile, I did. Based on my previous experience, I really wanted to hear the office lady's response, you know, the lady who yelled at me. It evidently did not go well when she called, because she told me to drop it.

These were not the only decisions they felt they could take over in my life. When enrolling at a local university, they took over all paperwork. My English Literature degree became Education without my approval. I tried to fight it and explain that it wasn't my degree, but they did not hear me.

When I said, "I don't want to teach," they misunderstood.

It wasn't so much that I didn't want to teach. I couldn't see myself, having just spent four years at a student's desk, flipped in the other direction as a teacher. I could not see myself in charge of a room of teenagers, especially considering I was not in charge of much of anything right now. When one is treated as a child, it is hard to make any progress toward adulthood.

My dad started screaming, "I don't want to go to work either, but you just go and do it."

He clearly did not understand that I wasn't saying I changed my mind. All this time, they thought I was going into Education.

As the career counselor explained, "Switching to Education added three years to my already two completed years of college. It would have been faster to finish my Bachelor's in Literature and get a Master's in Education through the Alternative Certification program because Kentucky teachers need a masters in five years anyway."

How could I have explained this to a parent who doesn't hear me, who cannot see past their own lens of experiences?

Instead, I snidely remarked, "I need a job," at the counselor.

Because I did.

How could I continue three more years of courses I did not want, all general education requirements with no more English courses that I loved so much?

For this reason, I think I fought my future desire to complete an Education program after being an adjunct for so long. I wanted to help struggling students, especially special needs children like my autistic son, but I fought this desire, thinking I was following a path that was required and expected of me, unsure whether this was truly what I wanted or whether I was simply being obedient.

After moving in with my husband, I transferred to another college, finished my Bachelor's in Literature, then a Masters in British Literature. I started teaching college at 24 years old. I considered either a doctorate or an Education degree. It was advocating for my own children that led me to Education.

The Road Not Taken

Mary Ellen Miller was one of my all-time favorite professors. She was my creative writing teacher who taught me a lot about my writing voice, mainly focusing on revision, specifically where my writing was nothing more than a visualization of my thought processes before getting to my actual poem.

More often than not, artfulness did not start until midway down the page. She helped me understand how to speak in images through poetry, leaving the rest of the story for implication and analysis. Hint at the story, don't tell it fully. I had this horrible *Dear Reader* habit where I felt I needed to explain myself.

Our major semester project was writing a full poetry portfolio, sharing our work in literature circles, and then submitting individual works for publication. I ended up publishing in a small local magazine, the Virginia Review, or something. Maybe Indiana. I forget exactly, but it was a publication that supported developing writers. Exposure. Not income.

She also arranged for a guest writer to speak at the university and offer a small workshop with her class. This is where I met Li-Young Lee, a Chinese American poet. He shared his work with us, reading both *Braiding* and *Persimmons*, his most well-known poem.

Braiding was a beautiful poem about his wife and their shared history together which was paralleled by the metaphor of braiding her hair. It was both hot and romantic, but sensual without being explicit.

Persimmons focused primarily on his life starting at grade school and continued into a discussion about his father whom he lost, but at the same time, it was about the role words played in our personal stories as well as heritage, told through images and the repetition of that Chinese apple, the persimmon.

As Professor Miller taught us, it told a story with images, and the story was done exceptionally well. I'm not embarrassed to admit that at 18 or 19, I was fairly enamored with Li-Young Lee.

After he read my poem, 'My Favorite Doll', he signed my copy of Rose, the Chapbook I purchased, "Robin, Fellow's poet, seer, sister, peace." I still have it shelved with the remainder of his poetry books, my favorite marked-up copy of 'Lady Chatterley's Lover', 'Mrs Dalloway' by Woolf, 'Madwoman in the Attic', 'Ariel' by Plath, T.S. Eliot's 'Wasteland' and other poems, and Bobbi Ann Mason's 'The Girl in the Blue Beret', and a handful of Tracey Chevalier novels.

When I get tipsy, I sometimes perform 'The Love Song of J. Alfred Prufrock' and transition into a creative explosion when my literary editor is turned off. Because, if my editor isn't turned off and placated with a little liquid courage, my poetry gets stomped on by concerns of appropriate word choice.

Later, as an adjunct faculty member, I had the pleasure of teaching his poem, 'Persimmons' to college Freshmen.

My Favorite Doll (2001)

The house still smelled of fresh-cut vegetables,
And the musk of an old woman

The lamps, jewelry boxes, pictures, tea sets,
Taken from the house.

More people went down the short hall,
To her room.

"She's not in there," I wanted to say.
But they all knew.
My mother knew all too well.

Her sewing box, dishes, pots, and candlesticks.
I watch them take apart her house.

My aunts hand me a doll.
Gray patches of faded blue flowers,
Tan mittened hands,
Sewn into obscure patterns.
With worn brown threads.

It's floppy head falls to my shoulder,
Golden yarn braids tickle my chin,

I cling to her,
My first smile all day,
My last memory of my Mimi,
Before the tubes in her wrists.

At the time I started college, I wanted to be a writer, so I started with a degree in creative writing. Professor Miller helped us chart out the writer's career, and it scared me. She showed us how to submit our work for publication and look at where to market the work using a copy of *The Writer's Market*.

I fell in love with the concept of writing for *The New Yorker* and maybe, pursuing a position as an editor for a publishing company. The idea of reading for a living and deciding what is published appealed to me, even though the path to get there was completely foreign.

Professor Miller told us if we could not plaster our bathroom in tiny form letter rejection slips that were typically no bigger than an index card, we could not call ourselves writers.

Again, this scared me. Putting myself out there as a writer sounded terrifying too. I saw myself in the company of great southern and Appalachian writers like Frank X. Walker, Silas House, and Bobbi Ann Mason—or rather, I would have liked to see myself in their company, but I simply didn't. I started looking at my writing differently.

I would get into frantic explosions of creativity, then nothing, so I would force it. In reviewing those explosions of creativity, I would see simply that, an explosion of words, and wonder if I am conveying what writing makes me feel. I don't believe I did.

I would get stalled on the appropriate words to say, then I'd wonder where I belong at all. Do my words have anything to say to anyone else but myself?

A writing career would take a long time to pursue to get to any financial stability, and I am too working class to wait. It is not like I'm any Raymond Carver.

I came from a family that looked at pursuing college as a luxury, and that the priority was to work. Once I graduated college, if I was not getting jobs easily and making bank, I clearly wasted four or more years going to school, and getting into debt, when I could have pursued an entry-level job, gained work experience, a paycheck, and seniority.

Full of High Sentence 2018

In my dirty white collar,
Above my raisin',
Looking down my nose,
Too good to work,
To get my hands dirty,
To make an honest living.

Wasting time finding myself,
Paying money instead of,
Accumulating hours,
For worthless degrees,

Pension, retirement, seniority,

Nose in a book,

Being lazy anti-social,
Living in a world outside of reality,
A dream,
But in a bad way.

What can you do with that?

I should've been a carpenter.

When I made the Dean's List after my first semester of college, I was eager to show my dad the letter. He was in the garage sorting some products for the store. He and Number Two decided to open a collectible store because she had a love of Barbies.

With the Beanie Baby craze coinciding with the opening of their business, the store continued successfully for a handful of years and offered me a part-time job throughout high school and into college.

When I showed him the letter, he screamed at me, "What, you expect something for this now? You should be thanking me for the opportunity to go to college."

It was an odd exchange. It let the wind completely out of my sails, and I shriveled up. But it wasn't the first time he voiced problems with paying for tuition, then housing, then the required food plan, and making too much for financial aid.

I imagine, while we were not poor, the additional expense of my college education was putting a strain on their finances or at least created bitterness that; I cost him money like when I needed a field trip fee or clothing, an unnecessary expense to him.

While he, also had the opportunity to go to school, I sometimes wondered if my success in school was a bone of contention for him since he failed, got a child pregnant, and had to quit. I often wondered if he wanted me to fail, or assumed I would, because he did.

He was too competitive to want to be outshined, especially by someone who did not follow in his footsteps or did as one is told. He was the type of parent who would rather be needed than watch his children become self-sufficient. If we were, this independence would be gobbled up by his upbringing rather than anything we did for ourselves.

Making the Dean's List was not the weirdest reason I got in trouble while in college though. For a writing course, I took the VHS tape 'Snow White and the Seven Dwarves' from my, or rather as I was later told the family's, collection to watch the documentary of animation to use as a source for a paper.

When returning for the weekend, I was thoroughly lectured about what they called theft because I dared take my all-time favorite Disney movie I was given for my birthday when I was little. Of all the things to get in trouble for in college, I dare take a cartoon movie to watch in the dorm. Let's all clutch our pearls.

Arguing the movie was clearly mine, I was told the movie collection was the family's not mine even if they were gifts because, a phrase repeated ad nauseam, they were worth money.

Evidently, we had the scandalous phallic symbol covers or something silly about collecting. I don't know. Many of the movies, like the old live-action movie Beauty and the

Beast from the mini-series long before Hermione starred in it, were gifts from Pops, Stephen's father, who loved getting us movies all the time.

When the movies were not from Pops, they were the main birthday gift I was given that year from my dad, but it was clear, just like my drum set or Tupperware they liked, things I had if they wanted them were theirs.

That year, during Black Friday sales, I bought myself a DVD player in order to start replacing my entire Disney movie collection I had lost as the VHS tapes sat collecting dust and decomposing in an outdoor storage shed with no temperature regulations, unused and unwanted; but are worth money one day, requiring that this Disney Princess could not have her birthday gifts.

It is easy to say, I did not pursue a writing career because of my blue-collar background and pressure from family, but it is more than that. It was fear. My own fear. Fear of failing at something.

I ended up switching to the study of literature, instead of writing because I would be able to scoop up the courses in creative writing and put them into English electives for a bachelor's in English Literature.

I did not fully understand what to do with an English degree at the time, but as I was told often when discussing college, "Go to college and pursue classes you enjoyed and a career you've never considered will be revealed."

It was like magic, and I believed it. I would find out about the world in college and career paths would be clearer to understand. I would find a way to use my study of literature.

Motherhood

A little girl, with long cartoon character-colored red hair, came into my classroom with larger holes in her pants, a pattern I recognized well. The pants were cut in a certain way which allowed her growing body to still put them on even though the clothes were ill-fitting and clearly uncomfortable.

She was an angry, fiery young lady who clearly exerted control in the classroom due to not having control of anything else in her life. Almost the entire front of the pant legs was cut completely out and the only thing that held her body into the pants were the strings from the frayed fibers of the denim over the large cutout holes.

The frayed fibers were cutting off her circulation, leaving white lines in her skin, and she would pull them to stretch it slightly. She was clearly in pain.

I am happy to say at this particular school, I did not have to dress code her. What many people forget when dress-coding young ladies is that they are not being inappropriate or dressing promiscuously and advertising an hourly rate. They are showing poverty, and an inability to get the right clothes as their bodies grow.

Daisy Dukes was not a sexy fashion trend. It was a necessity for young southern women to continue to wear clothes that fit their waist but not their legs, so cutting them up to one's nether regions was a necessity.

When I was little, some girls at school showed me how to use safety pins and rubber bands to connect the button on my pants to the buttonhole on the other side when the button did not reach.

Please understand when I say this, I was not impoverished. The necessity of buying appropriate clothing was not something my single dad who lived among 10 brothers and sisters thought about or valued.

I remember a middle school math teacher sending a letter home to my dad about my midriff. I was scandalized that this teacher was telling me I was showing a private part of which I was unaware.

When in reality, I was growing breasts and taller, which meant my shirt did not reach the top of my pants. What I also did not understand was why this meant I was in trouble.

I went to the counselor about this red-haired, mean-spirited young girl with ill-fitting clothes, asking if someone could simply take her clothes shopping because clearly, she just needed someone to be a mother to her.

For my birthday, when I was in third grade, my mother took me clothes shopping for the first time in my life. I was having a birthday party, and she took me to the mall to pick out a nice dress. It was overwhelming. Girls' sizes were stupid and inconsistent due to different brands, and sizes for women versus juniors did not make any sense.

I did not fully understand what to do, because like I said, this was the first time in my life I picked out clothes.

Normally, with two older sisters, I had plenty of hand-me-downs, but as we all grew, clothes became interchangeable and then simply disappeared into someone else's closet. My mom wanted the selection of the outfit to be completely my decision, so she gave me little guidance.

I was so afraid of making the wrong decision that I marched her to every store and tried on numerous outfits before deciding on a little teal, white, black, and brown skirt and matching top. The top was button-down and tied off at the end at the waist.

The skirt was super cute with fringe trim at the seams and a southwestern print. My mom was growing tired and frustrated, because of how long I had taken, and when she retold the story; she went on about how much time of hers I wasted.

Wasting an adult's time seemed to be the theme of my childhood. After my sisters moved in with my mother, it was brought to light how thoroughly the parenting job was outsourced to them.

Once, when my mom drove me to school one Monday morning before she went to work, she inadvertently missed the announcement that my school was having a two-hour delay due to snow, so she dropped me off at the door of the elementary school and drove away from the empty parking lot.

Fortunately, the door was open, and the secretary found me, terrified, walking along the color-coded floor of the empty school building that was, at the time, reminiscent of a Freddy Krueger movie for me.

When I told my mom about what had happened, she laughed and said, "Oh, darn, we could have gone out for donuts."

I was irritated that she didn't pay attention and was not concerned, but in the back of my mind, I wondered if this was intentional, because she had to go to work and knew someone would be there at the school to compensate. But I don't know.

She did ask me occasionally, what grade I was in, so there was no guarantee she knew the school's name or the county in which I attended school.

Sometimes, without a mother, I felt like I did not know how to be a girl. I was raised by a man who taught me pink is stupid, Barbies are overpriced dolls with the same face, and that girlie meant deficient in some way, lacking in personal strength, physically and mentally.

Number Two teased my dad the year he bought me a bike. She said, "But it's pink."

And my dad said, "Yeah, she's a girl."

"But not a pink girl."

I was clearly not.

In high school, I would try to invite my mom into my life, but she was always uninterested. The trip to my town wasn't worth the effort. I invited her to football games because I was involved in the marching band.

I was in the drum line and got to march in the New Year's Eve parade in Paris, France around Sacré-Cœur, The Basilica of the Sacred Heart. The marching band was important to me, like a second family, a place to go because-as I said before—I wasn't welcome at home. When I had a solo playing the quads, I made sure I told her but again, not interested.

I started the song 'Joy to the World' with a quads solo. Normally, I played snare, but they moved me to squads for one of our rotating shows, so it was a big deal to me. Quads are four drums strapped to my chest with a harness and functioned like a drum set.

My 5.4-foot-tall pound self could hardly move with the drums across my shoulders, but for one show, I got to play the quads.

My mom's reason for this disinterest wasn't necessarily because she did not want to see my show. She said she hated football and didn't want to sit through the game, so on senior night when proud parents marched their children down the field in celebration, she was still disinterested and insulted that I would put her in a situation where she would be near and photographed with my father.

I remember this fact when she volunteered for the training camp for a football team. Rationalizing it, I remembered it was a big social thing with her girlfriends, but it still boils down to the fact that she was uninterested in me, a waste of her time, just like the little third grader's dress.

When I told her I was joining the theater, she immediately said she would go if I had a big part like the lead or something; because she didn't want to drive all the way there if I was the curtain puller.

The irony was I wasn't inviting her, and I was actually the curtain puller and helped with the costumes, where I got the opportunity to coat my friend's bright white legs with make-up for the play 'Guys and Dolls'.

Turns out, I have trouble reading aloud and did not like trying out for parts because no matter how much I practiced, I could never fluently read the script once I looked down at the words. The only reason I joined was because all my friends were in the play.

Her disinterest in me, made me very bitter and resentful, so I would pray for my mother, but it started consuming me with rage as a teenager. The daily talk with God about getting a parent who did not want me was a challenge and would trigger me often.

It would make me dwell on unwanted memories, so I finally took it up to Mary's intercession. I stared up at her beautiful statue, that serene smile, kind eyes, and open hands, surrounded by the blue cloak.

We made a deal, Mary and I, that I would stop praying for my mother if she would take over those prayers for me. It hurts too much, to daily think about being so unwanted and unconnected with a parent. This simmered some of the rage.

It wasn't until I had my own children that I realized my mom, as young as she was, kind of stopped progressing emotionally. She was perpetually that 14-year-old girl who stopped her education at around eighth grade.

How could I expect a person to understand me when my own experiences are so foreign to her? She never even made it to high school.

Thus, motherhood for me was found in different faces, in the face of Mary as Jesus said on the cross, "Woman, behold, your son."

Then he said to the disciple, "Behold, your mother."

And from that hour the disciple took her into his home (John 19:25-27). Through this, Jesus gave us Mary as our mother as well as his own. Growing up without a mother, Mary as my mother appealed to me. Other Marian accounts through scripture illustrated many things about womanhood to me.

When the Angel Gabriel requested Mary's permission to carry God's son, she said, "Behold, I am the handmaid of the Lord. May it be done to me according to your word" (Luke 1:38).

Her yes was scandalous if one considers the implications. She did not run to her parents or her betrothed to seek permission or to explain the situation, God's request of her.

She simply and eagerly agreed to God's word, knowing that it would work out, even though, as Joseph's dream indicated, could have resulted in her stoning, and most likely did result in rumors and a poor reputation.

Further research into the saints as well as the Marian apparitions also indicated scandalous women who stood up for themselves and their mission and purpose.

St Dymphna fled her crazy father who looked for a woman as beautiful as her mother who died only to find his own daughter.

St Thérèse of Lisieux, the little flower who encouraged those to come to God with the love and devotion of a child; marched to Rome to argue with the pope that he should amend the rules and allow her to enter the covenant, a year early, according to her calling.

She also wrote a beautiful novel, filled with poetic writing that explained the beauty of God's love and the mystery of our own purpose explained through natural imagery.

If one considers the implication, celibacy and the taking of a religious vow is a complete rejection of the domestic sphere and the marriage market in which women are often sold because they have rejected motherhood and marriage, scandalous.

Probably, a very different take than for those who have followed a life of obedience to God. But like Mary, the handmaid of the Lord, that yes was still the exertion of the free will God has given.

Kaye, who taught Catechism class and later, became my son's godmother and my confirmation sponsor, stepped in as a mother as well. I remember how she helped me get ready for my first dance when I was in eighth grade, the day my niece, Summer's first child was born.

Kaye helped me get ready in a beautiful velvety dress and put crystal barrettes in my curled-up hair. As my dad pointed out, my ex-boyfriend's mother was a mother figure who was there for me often.

Jessie's mother mothered me too. She even offered me her wedding dress. Many women loved me and took me into their lives.

Teachers, like Phyllis Schlich, also stepped in and played a role in parenting me. Mrs Schlich was a wonderful English teacher who was married to a school counselor, ironically enough. She formed a creative writing club that met early in the morning before school started.

It was perfect because it allowed me to leave the house before Number Two woke up and gave me a reason to be at school after school was over to do something constructive; to work on like the literary magazine.

Sometimes, I would drive my car with the windows frosted over blindly and park 7 to 10 houses down the street while my car defrosted, so my existence in their house would not somehow get me in trouble due to whatever mood Number Two awoke.

Mrs Schlich took us to the Carnegie Center where we met with published authors and worked on creative writing prompts. Her house was open to the creative writing club, she allowed me to bring my drum set, and she threw us a party.

After I graduated, she turned the club into a credit-earning creative writing course. She, like Grams, opened doors to understanding a new perspective and a variety of life experiences, another lens through which to look. It was no surprise that after she retired, she immediately returned to teaching, but did so overseas in Turkey. She is an amazing woman, who showed me I was worth her time.

Grams, toward the end of her life, lost most of her hearing and needed a feeding tube. I am happy to say, before she passed she met my husband who she immediately loved. She told me he was the right choice because I needed someone as smart as me who thought like me, someone who would share in my dreams.

My mom refused Hospice but got so upset with Grams being there in her house, bitter that she had to take care of her, and mentioned often she wanted her to go ahead and die. Care for Grams transitioned to Stephen's brother, Jerry. Grams died one day, alone at her house, while Jerry was at work.

Unloved and unwanted, resented for being sick and dying. She was quietly cremated. No one told me where they laid the ashes, but I hope it was at Bernheim Forest.

When I graduated college with my bachelors, Eastern Kentucky University inconsiderately scheduled the graduation for the big University of Kentucky and the University of Louisville basketball game.

My mom and Stephen could not make it, but as they said, "It's not like you finished anything. You moved from one thing to the other."

EKU was clearly inconsiderate not realizing the importance of the UK's big basketball game with an in-state rival. It was a much bigger deal than my graduation, and since my dad wasn't currently speaking to me, they did not have the competition with my dad to pressure them to attend.

I was encouraged to also not invite my sisters since I would still be going to school after graduation, and then I was berated for going to school to study a field that wasn't real like nursing. Also, for so long instead of finishing so quickly like Autumn, who had graduated with an Associates in Nursing.

My mom could list the credentials, majors, academic scholarships, and achievements of Mark Pope and other basketball players, but could not understand the reason why Autumn finished her associates before I finished my masters degrees.

It irked me. A Lot. So, the irony of my mom's request for pictures of all of us receiving our master's degree once my sisters and niece graduated wasn't lost on my husband who had to hear me roar with bitter laughter. Summer graduated with a Masters in Nursing after her business degree.

Autumn graduated with a masters, and then a Doctorate in Nursing. Rayne graduated with an associates which led her to a position as a secretary for the F.B.I. Not that these accomplishments should not be celebrated and praised, because they clearly should be.

But why was I such a disappointment? Why did my accomplishments not matter until someone else did it? I just wasn't important.

While there was a huge disinterest in my life, I knew my mother loved me. I was just a foreigner in her world. How do I expect a woman who did not make it to high school to understand her daughter who taught college and currently teaches high school? I am very much a stranger in a strange land when it comes to conversations with her.

While I would love to talk about my career and what was going on in my life, our conversations revolve around parenting and cordial greetings of love for each other.

Some of the best memories I have of my mom are watching her clean the house while listening to Prince and Billy Idol and watching episodes of 'Quantum Leap and Highlander' together, sharing with her things she enjoyed.

After I complained about not knowing how to raise children once, we found out Christian has autism, and voicing the fear around such a revelation, she said, "You are doing fine as a mom. Christian knows you love him and that is all that matters."

So, I must remember, she did fine as a mom because I know she loves me.

Ungrateful

He is very careful and loving and hardly lets me stir without special direction. I have a scheduled prescription for each hour in the day; he takes all care from me, and so I feel basely ungrateful not to value it ·more.
 - Charlotte Perkins Gilman, 'The Yellow Wallpaper'

Historically, due to the lesser social status of women, those of the female gender have been denigrated with this term of gratefulness.

The first social services program in the United States was created for the prosperity of widows and orphans due to the lack of opportunity for women to procure their livelihood within the perimeters of Capitalism.

Thus, this basic livelihood provided to them, in their beggar status, is something for which they must be grateful.

And these women, due to the death of their husbands, must be the worthy poor as well, those untouched by the cruelty of poverty somehow as they live in this grueling fight for survival.

The worthy poor. The very, very worthy
And beautiful poor. Perhaps just not too swarthy? Perhaps,
just not too dirty, nor too dim, nor—passionate
- Gwendolyn Brooks, 'The Lovers of the Poor'

As I mentioned before, there were four years when I had no contact with my dad. Within those four years, I finished my bachelors and my first master's degree, and had my second child. Also, found out my oldest had Pervasive Development Disorder: Not Otherwise Specified or PDD-NOS, which later, turned into a full diagnoses of autism.

I received speech services for my son through *First Steps* and started teaching college at 24 years old. So, there was a special type of rage watching my dad brag about his brilliant daughter; as if he contributed in some way to the path I blazed out for myself instead of becoming one of the various obstacles. But I've always been skilled at vaulting.

Money is what ultimately led to the dissolution of our relationship temporarily.

It is not easy realizing that the person who is typically in your corner, your cheerleader in your life, has been all this time wanting you to fail because you did not do what you were told to do.

Everything in your life was a punishment for being a disobedient daughter, and your success flies in the face of that believed cosmic karmic debt God owed my parents for the choices I made.

And my failure needs to be a recognition of my need for their support. Even though the support, financially or otherwise, always costs more than I can afford—my choices.

Since my dad continued to offer financial support in one way or another, I decided against my better judgment to accept his continuous offers to help. He was already disappointed that Hilary and I eloped, and my dad didn't get the opportunity to walk me down the aisle.

However, I did invite him and Number Two to bless our marriage, which his wife did not attend but he did. He gave us a check for $300, offering more financial support if we needed it but grumbling about how he thought I'd have a real wedding.

Since things were awkward at the moment and the wedding was rather quick considering they threw me out, I was more interested in a marriage than another awkward celebration with both parents who struggled to share the same physical space with one another. As guests discussed the futility of unions in general because of their own failed relationships, taking bets on the length of the arrangements.

I don't understand why my sisters kept planning uncomfortable events for their children that involved both parents. I suggested they consider another option because my dad is socially awkward and prefers private celebrations, while my mom is more social and likes to host.

I was told, "You are the one who makes a big deal about it."

It was always awkward. Since my dad was awkward, he would as I call it *show his ass*. Once during a skating party for my niece, my dad got overly competitive with Number Two during a race.

He was skilled at roller skating and tried to tease his wife during the race by quickly skating backward in front of her. However, she easily maneuvered around him since he had to slow down slightly.

He did this weird turn flipping around quickly and sped up to pass her, but turned too quickly and fell to the ground, breaking his wrist so badly they had to put metal screws inside his skin to connect the bones.

Afterward, he vowed to never skate, but in reality, he should've vowed to stop being competitive and careless.

Another time at a pool party, mom stormed off early because my dad tossed one of their grandchildren in the water who had been peacefully floating on a floaty.

I yelled at him about not knowing whether the particular child could swim, and he joked, "It's just one of them. They can just make another."

He often made loud, silly comments that he knew would annoy Mom. Even now, I think he so desperately wants her to see him. Parties were spent moving from one group awkwardly to another, watching them keep a distance and glare occasionally.

I decided to accept my dad's offer of financial help after my husband was furloughed as a book manager due to a lack of sales. Barnes and Noble had to reconfigure everything due to the rise of the popularity of Amazon. He came home from work one day, and I was lying in our bed, roughly six months pregnant.

He was scared when he came in, knelt beside the bed next to me, and cried as he slowly explained they let him go as he was the last manager hired.

It was scary at first, but we came up with a plan. I encouraged him to pursue his dreams and return to college, knowing he never wanted to stay at a job like that anyway.

We decided to finish out our rental contract and move into family housing on campus.

I told my dad about our financial troubles and the cost of some of the outstanding bills, and he generously offered to pay everything after he came to take Christian for the weekend. When he returned with my son, he would take me to pay the bills personally, so it sounded like the visit with Christian was the cost of the loan.

I acquiesced, even though I hated handing off my child but had I said no, I would be ungrateful. During the visit, Christian got really sick with a stomach bug, but I wasn't informed until my son was returned to me.

My dad, then, did not just pay the bills, he walked me around stores like a disobedient child as he lectured me about spending, going through purchases, and lecturing me about decisions I made in front of people as we closed out accounts.

One clerk even said, "There is no guarantee she cannot just reopen the account and max it out again," feeding into the narrative he was creating publicly.

When I got home, my dad pulled Hilary aside to discuss the payment plan which was outlandish. My dad wasn't generously helping up; he was extending his line of credit to us which we were to start paying immediately at the end of the month which was only two weeks away.

Hilary gently explained that while the loan was reasonable and generous; it was not feasible based on the plans he and I had made. We were going to spend a few weeks in Florida with his grandmother until we needed to start moving into the family house on campus because we both were going to finish our degrees.

My dad laughed at us and said we were being irresponsible, explaining college was a luxury that we didn't have anymore because we had a family to raise and owed him money. So when my dad brags about my accomplishments, I desperately want to remind him that he told me to work instead of going back to school twice; once when I was told to work at Toyota and now.

Blue Vs. White

Sometimes, an inability to hear and see,
is a choice,
Shows what one has deemed unimportant.

I used to get upset that my degrees make no sense,
There isn't a cash-in value for them,
Only a delay in work,
And the work gained in exchange for the degree,
Doesn't sound real,
Or important,
Or sound like anything at all really,
Or doesn't exchange for the time spent pursuing the degree in the first place?

And it is competitive.
You cannot just get that amazing job at graduation,
You work toward it, in the same way you worked toward that degree.

And this progress to some looks like a failure,
Due to its lack of immediacy.

So, it is just easier.
To make those white collars value-less,
Unimportant,
Unseen, unheard.

Because a degree a person gets,
Is not something that was available,
Tangible,
Achievable.

To the entry-level worker.
If it was, you'd never be happy in the place you are.
That entry-level job had value,
That work was important,

And it led to other things. Until it dries up.
You, at the mercy of that company,
Your financial security opened and closed with their doors.
And I can take my degree elsewhere. And open up any door I want.
You, standing on the hill, while we climb mountains. That aren't even visible behind your lens.
But you get that paycheck, and it keeps you afloat long enough to feel a little more important lording it over people as they make progress.
But you feel you have *made it*. Until you don't,
Then you shake that fist in the air,
And blame some faceless entity for your situation,
Someone stole something the black person,
The illegal immigrant,
The millennial who won't work, The younger person,

The working mother who somehow was handed something
You never got.
All these other people,
Took
Something From
You.

Right?

But in reality, you were just utterly replaceable with another,
Young, abled-bodied body.
Because the factory broke you after 20+ years.

But yes, look down on me.
I must be at fault for your situation somehow.
My job doesn't look real to you,
Or hard enough for the income I get.

    Had I known the stipulations before the loan, I would never have made it.

    That night, I was taking care of a very sick little boy who was throwing up and had diarrhea. I had never seen him so sick, but in a day or so, he was fine. Unfortunately, for me, I was not. Due to the loss of fluids and the stress, I had to be hospitalized, having lost 10 pounds.

    I don't know why I took him up on the money. I knew it was stupid, but he was trying too hard to reconnect with us because he had been such a jerk when he tossed out my things on the porch. Maybe the money was his way to make amends because that is how he does things. Gifts and money are manipulated.

I thought we could have a good relationship and he would help us out, as long as I didn't bring up how he mistreated me during my pregnancy when he took the food stamps I was illegally receiving.

Things didn't improve, so I wrote a thoughtful letter outlining his wrongs. I expressed my feelings of helplessness during my pregnancy with Christian, especially the deep hunger I felt.

His response was a single letter saying, "I'll read this every day to remember what a bad daddy I had been."

In order to paint a horrible picture of me which impacted relationships with other family members, he told people I stole from him which should not have surprised me. His fabricated stories about himself have always only had a small kernel of truth.

He gloats about how he paid for Summer's furniture because she made an irresponsible decision and couldn't pay for it. However, he leaves off that she picked the pretty furniture she wanted and paid payments on them.

He was so upset about paying her payments, that he offered to buy them as a gift. Funny, how it turns into, he claims she did something irresponsible when in reality, he offered to pay for something. That's how his gifts and help work, a reminder of his might and our own smallness.

He also gloats about saving Memaw's farm that she almost lost because she was dumb enough, in his words, to put all her medical bills on a credit card instead of paying the bills in payments directly through the hospital.

I'm not sure how true this story is, because even though he was talking about his own mother; the message was an illustration of how smart he was with money and how irresponsible his own mother had been.

I wouldn't be surprised if he somehow got his family's farm from his mother through this little scheme if any of it was true in the first place. While my dad was successful enough, he was always envious of the amount of land my grandfather accumulated, a feat he could never claim.

My dad may have been a douche, but he was still my dad, so I tried to keep the lines of communication open. Unconditional love, I guess, wasn't my dad's strong suit.

He can easily throw someone away for not obeying him or even disagreeing with him. That is why he throws his children out, gets divorced, and has no friendships outside of family. His love is conditional.

During this time, we found out that Christian's speech issue was due to autism or PDD-NOS, so I included my dad and Number Two in a family newsletter updating everyone about Christian's diagnoses. My dad made no acknowledgment of this nor of any of the Christmas cards I sent throughout the years.

When Autumn's son turned one, I had to go to her party and watch my children, one of whom my dad had never met, be ignored by my dad in full display of my mom, sisters, my aunts, and cousins on my dad's side.

It was uncomfortable, embarrassing, and humiliating. I remember eating quickly and nervously, wondering how long I needed to stay to show my sister the appropriate amount of love and support before I ran for the car.

It must've been noticeable because my aunt gave me this strange look—*you must be hungry*—because I had been shoveling and inhaling the food.

I laughed, playing it off that toddlers keep me so busy that I have to eat fast, and then that pit in my stomach turned, that worthless feeling again. The memory of not being worth the food you eat.

When throwing away my plate, Number Two slipped into the kitchen to quietly and secretly thank me for including them in the newsletter about Christian.

My stomach was still turning, so I just kind of blinked at her, not sure how to respond or if I even wanted to. I think I squeaked out an okay. It felt like a trick because remember, this is the woman who said if she had grounds, she would take Christian from me.

Then, she apologized for how she treated me growing up which was incredibly odd, not just the apology but for the blanketed vagueness of it, definitely an apology from someone who thought sins did not have to be vocalized and specified to be forgiven.

I wondered if she sat up late hurt by a comment, she hurled at me years ago like I did. Was she thinking about standing over me while I ate, lecturing me about my bowl of macaroni and cheese?

Did she see the confused little girl about 10 or 11 trying to wipe the streaks of Windex off the bathroom mirror as she yelled and called her stupid for not knowing how to do something properly?

Clearly, she was on her way out and was mending some fences. It was the last time I saw her because they got a divorce. After my dad's divorce, my husband said I could not send him a card of congratulations. It would have been perceived as in poor taste, but I was actually happy for him.

These were the kinds of people who magnified the worst out of each other. They would fuel a hatefulness in each other like a game, so I thought with her gone, maybe I could reconnect with my dad.

Hilary had sent my dad an email, requesting a payment plan on the loan, but my dad said, "I don't take money from my daughters."

Clearly an attack on my husband directly.

That year, my dad had won the lottery, not the full lottery but a partial one with co-workers at Toyota, so he took my sisters and their children to Disney. This wasn't the first time my dad won the lotteries.

He has a minor gambling issue that seems to have led him to run businesses that are just cluttered storage spaces filled with items he bought; because they were good deals, even if they aren't worth much now.

Nothing is a bigger waste of money than having so much that a person cannot find what they want when they want it. I'll never find that damn Christening Gown.

Number Two started working at Toyota after they closed their business once the Beanie Baby craze fizzled out; meaning they filed taxes as having sold things at cost, paid off my dad's loans in products, and bankrupted the business.

According to rumor, Number Two wanted to get a boob job which my dad thought was ridiculously stupid and unnecessary. When my dad started getting uncomfortable with his current wife, he followed her home and found her in their bed with another man, again according to rumor.

They divorced, but the other man didn't want her either, so she asked my dad to take her back. I don't believe this story for a minute because I know my dad. He would never have allowed her to bury her dog on his property if she had cheated.

They would never stay cordial afterward. I know that a cheating woman makes him look like the victim. No one faults him for leaving a cheating woman. No one claims that he failed at another marriage.

But what most likely happened was he is just unbearable, and behind closed doors without at least another person to keep him in check, he can be a dangerous man.

After I left, he was alone with her. He could have easily gotten rid of her, which might have led to a costly divorce settlement or domestic violence charges against him.

Around Christmas, I got a weird message from him saying he had gifts for us, which was odd because after four years, he had yet to even acknowledge my second child at all, but now he had gifts. I could tell someone had baked things and made care packages.

Turns out not long after the divorce, my dad started dating this really nice lady, named Sue, who secretly moved in with him. They collected elephants together. I guess he was too ashamed to tell her we weren't speaking, so we had to act like everything was perfectly normal, and we weren't estranged.

As he carried in armloads of things for the family, we hugged and greeted each other, but I stood off at a distance and observed him, not knowing what to do. Hilary was nice enough to take the lead and introduce our youngest to my dad.

Not knowing what to call him, Hilary introduced my dad in a very odd formal title of *Grandpa Gus, your mom's dad*, and from now onwards, my kids called my dad, *Grandpa Gus*, as determined and named by my husband.

My brilliant little four-year-old looked confused and said, "Where've you been?"

Then, she offered my dad a knuckle sandwich and all was well.

After meeting Sue a few times, going on family outings, and rejecting offers to take the kids to Disney, my dad started his plan to retire from Toyota. Within that plan, he ends up dumping Sue due to the fear of taking on her medical debt because it would eat into his retirement.

Sue had been born with her intestines outside of her body, so she has had numerous procedures throughout her life including surgeries, the upkeep of such conditions, and all that entails.

My dad said, "As old as she is, she should have planned better."

She had to go into medical bankruptcy.

Not long after ending the relationship, he started up with this other lady, the implication of the beginning of their relationship suggested some overlap with his involvement with both ladies.

This other lady, Ruth, is now his current wife, who I believe is a good choice for him. She worked at Toyota, thus, he has the proper respect for her as she has followed what he believes to be the appropriate path in a superior company with the right kind of benefits.

Unlike him, she did not move out of the holler. Instead, like my grandfather, she accumulated property in his hometown of Bardstown/New Haven, and she knew all his family having grown up with them.

Ironically, before her mother was married, her mom dated my grandfather. Thus, my dad could value what she did with her life while also stepping into her paid-for house and property quietly.

When I met her, I immediately liked her because she said, "When I met your daddy, I thought to myself, you were that perv who went after little Rose," in her thick southern accent with the mean-spirited but good-natured sense of humor.

We were going to get along just fine. She is very motherly with my dad too, which is nice because I think my dad struggles with basic life skills. So, it was great to hear she could cook and bake his favorite cakes. That way, he didn't have to win the cakes once a year at the cakewalks at the church picnic.

Before they got married, she wanted to meet me privately, take me out to dinner, and bond. I'm embarrassed to admit that I vomited too much about my dad after someone incorrectly stated that I didn't go to Disney on family trips the year he won the lottery, all because I'm protective of Christian.

He clearly did not want to admit that he stopped talking to me and went on a trip with his other daughters. So, I unloaded on her like a gun all the information about our temporary estrangement, why that happened, how much of a total douche my dad was, and how he could very well be a danger to her if she wasn't careful,

While she was startled, she was fascinated too, interested in what insight I had about the man she was going to marry and how many lies he had been telling her about himself she had been slowly uncovering.

Being Catholic as well, I told Ruth that she had grounds for divorce due to how he misrepresented himself to her which could negate his and her ability to make a vow to one another. Evidently, when my niece had her baby, he had failed to mention to Ruth that his grandchild was pregnant.

He told her it was an embarrassing topic, but she reminded him that a baby was a baby, and he didn't have room to talk. I really liked her. I knew she wasn't going to take his shit, so I made sure, she was no longer out of the loop on a lot of unpleasant but necessary topics.

Not long after they were married, she got to see firsthand how horrible he treated me, because as she said, "I know they warned me at work how much of a jerk he is but I didn't realize it was this bad."

I really like Ruth. She isn't a groomed teenager financially tied to him. She isn't a single parent struggling to raise her child, looking for that white picket fence.

She is just living her life and wants to be with my dad, which makes me wonder how long this will last. The two previous relationships each lasted 12 years. Hilary and I are approaching 20 years old, something I remind him of when he gives marital advice.

I say, "Marital advice? Really from you?"

I once reminded my dad, when he had been yelling at Ruth for fluctuating on the gas pedal in a way he didn't like, "Ruth doesn't need you. She loves you. Treat her better."

Then, he pouted, and she had to go parent the situation. She functions as a good mediator between me and my dad. When I finally had to block him on Facebook for correcting me like a child for thoughts I had. He tagged his siblings for follow-up or taunted my mother under family pictures with comments like *must be in the genes*.

Ruth intervened between us, giving me the platform to explain to her without my dad's screaming rage and inability to hear me interrupting my thoughts.

I explained that his behavior online shows he cannot see me as an adult and there are things about my life and family that will go public that he will not be able to handle like my child coming out as transgender; thus, he and I need to separate our social media in order to function successfully in our relationship.

Suffice it to say, my dad and I need a country between us.

My Vulcan Baby

My dad called on my son's 18th birthday. I inadvertently failed to put my dad on speakerphone, a mistake that will not be made in the future.

When Christian got off the phone, he was chuckling to himself, so I asked, "What did he say?"

Christian said, "He told me I could move out if I wanted to."

This revelation clearly enraged me because my dad knew that we were applying for guardianship over our autistic son to keep him safe and to support him as he continued job placement and shadowing opportunities through the Department of Vocational Rehabilitation.

Noticing my change in demeanor, he followed up with a playful statement that had a note of superiority in his speech, "He clearly doesn't understand the situation."

We all laughed knowing Christian was right as he typically was, and I am reminded of the quote my philosopher friend shared with me once when venting about my father:

"Never attribute to malice that which is adequately explained by stupidity."

-Robert J. Hanlon.

Because Mars Wasn't Hiring

When I started writing, I did not know what it was I was writing: an article, a reflection, a journal, a story, and for what purpose, for what audience. But looking back at the piece, I realize it helped me to see myself differently, to see myself as a character with conflicts and resolutions like a book.

I became a hero in my text because I had never stopped to see myself as a resilient person. I never stopped to see the girl with the book and goals because I only saw the little girl standing on the sidewalk among the tulips—asking if we could just go. The helpless, powerless girl with the 'Clan of the Cave Bear' hair, still asking Daddy for permission. But dammit, I'm 40 years old.

I started writing when I was in the middle of professional development in a new school, a new department, and learning a new system of writing instruction, and all I was feeling was isolated and out of place.

These feelings of being lesser have followed me throughout my life, especially in connection with economic stability. I relived these feelings of worthlessness when my PTSD would be triggered by an inconsiderate, *I've worked all my life, people just need to work, pull up from your bootstraps* type of comment. The feeling in my stomach of hunger in particular.

I taught at a university when my family was on food stamps.

At the same university where when I discussed an article about Meritocracy, a student, who clearly had not read went on a tangent about her perspective on the Affordable Care Act and health care to anyone regardless of the type of job they held.

The student said something about how entitled people are and how they should *just find a better job*.

Just like a day or so ago, I held my tongue because I had a strong desire to say, "Well, I'm trying."

But I did not, knowing that there may be ramifications to my position. The last thing I needed was for my department chair to get a call from a Republican donor who didn't want his baby to be taught by a working-class woman who didn't make enough money to have appropriate health care.

There is a sense of shame that goes along with not having enough money like you've done something horribly wrong in your life.

The sad reality is that the young girl, who most likely had health insurance through her parents, believed that those with entry-level jobs do not deserve the insurance. Those folks are in lower-paying jobs, and it's super important for them to have a stable job with benefits—especially if they end up dealing with stuff like cancer, pregnancy, or any other health issues that might come up in life.

Yes, laughable, I know! Heaven forbid someone in their 20s get cancer.

Once I realized that my job as an adjunct college professor would not be the stepping stone into academia I had hoped and that being a professor did not allow me to help struggling learners, I decided to pursue a second Master's Degree in Education through the Alternative Certification Process at the same university where I taught.

I did consider getting a doctorate but realized this was a less marketable choice and could limit my husband's career decisions. He is currently employed as a social worker.

Unsurprisingly, these feelings of being out of place crawled out of me when I was in college, as a student and an adjunct faculty, impostor syndrome I believe it was they call it.

Lashbrook, a great supervillain name, was another adjunct member and a professor who, for whatever reason, disliked me immensely. She, like me, held a master's degree but had decades of teaching experience at the public school level.

She would get frustrated with me often and say things like, "Why don't you already know this? You've been in education."

I would remind her that my masters was in British Literature, so expecting me to understand educational theory and academic standards prior to taking an education course was unreasonable.

Maybe *for whatever reason* was clearer to me than I realize now that I think about it. Authoritative titles have never meant much to me, especially when there was such a clear and noticeable gap in knowledge.

That was clear with Lashbrook. She was a scattered professor, scanned papers for errors instead of content, and wrote hateful feedback in the margins about how we should know better. Oftentimes, as I pointed out directly to her, her comments were incorrect, her grammar was dated, and her *college skim* was not effective.

Punctuation can have a subjective quality. She would mark a fragment and miss the fact that I was directly quoting something in fragment form, thus, her lecture on an incomplete sentence was not only unwarranted but needlessly nasty and only showed that she did not read the paper.

These encounters were not indicative of my entire experience at the college. The majority of the professors were eager to help and support future educators.

Unfortunately, Lashbrook was in charge of clinical and observational placements. She placed me with a gentleman who taught Advanced Placement English and whose last name was printed on every train throughout the town. His family was kind of a big deal.

As he told me during my clinical, Lashbrook said that I was only there to observe, so I wasn't his student to support because that was my professor's job, and I was not going to take over his class.

AP testing is a big deal, and he did not want me to interfere with his students' scores by wasting their time with my instructional practice. He was not incorrect though. AP testing is a big deal and requires additional AP testing professional development.

It was a miserable experience because for my clinical college class, I had to ask him to mentor and support me during assignments, and I was to teach multiple lessons in his room.

Lashbrook said there was a bit of a mix-up and changed my clinical focus to my teaching style at the college level. But he also pointed out that watching someone like him was super valuable since he's got perfect academic language and diction, and I could really use that as a model. I totally got where he was coming from.

I. Talk. Funny. It is colloquial in a lot of ways, but it was also my accent. And it said, I am not from here, academia, and it was somehow written on me.

When she observed me, I made sure to wear my rebellion infinity scarf. Summer's scarf actually. I swiped it from her after she bought it and pleaded with her, in a way only a little sister can, for the scarf.

It was an oversized scarf in black and white, very proper and appropriate for the situation, but looking closer, the lace made a repetitive pattern of skulls. This was my act of rebellion, my way of exerting authority and to make the statement the only way I could that looks can be deceiving.

This would not be my final run-in with this professor before ending my academic career. Lashbrook was assigned the Ruby Payne article on poverty for our online course instruction, and unfortunately, I don't think she understood it very well, but also the Payne article has a disturbing message, a classist one.

To start the lesson, Lashbrook said anecdotally, "I am surprised it was not talking about black people, because I always assumed it was black people, but in my research before this lesson, I found Payne was discussing her own in-laws."

It was an odd statement, an embarrassingly racist statement, and I told her. I also debated her comments about how the poor spent money.

Instead of understanding that the poor learned how to deal with less and they possess the *life is fleeting* concept, she simply stated the poor did not know how to use the money on things they really need—implying, if they saved their meager amount of money, living a life of thrift, they wouldn't be poor.

If they had a fridge, they'd sell it to go on a family vacation. The poor were loud because the television or radio was always on.

When I would call her on these gross oversimplifications, other students would correct me because they were in the field and saw the impacts of poverty on their students which was not my point.

Yes, poverty impacts people and alters their day-to-day interactions. It was the judgment placed on the observations with which I had issues. It was clearly class warfare, and this course, clearly had an agenda against the people in the situation—not the situation itself.

After the course, I left Lashbrook 'Whistling and Crowing: Women of Appalachian', a case study of Appalachian women's education and the socio-economic limitations and told her she should broaden her worldview. Like I said, I think I know very well why she did not like me.

While my accounts may make it sound like I had the upper hand, I had this constant feeling of being the *other*, lesser, an impostor. You don't belong here.

Or in my best southern accent that I have trained myself to lose by slowing my speech, "You ain't from around here, are you?"

While completing my education degree, my husband and I were learning a lot about our little boy. Christian did not speak much, and since he was my first baby, I didn't particularly find it peculiar until our doctor pointed it out at our wellness visit.

We were given a referral for First Steps with support from an occupational therapist and a speech pathologist. While Christian made enough sounds to be functional, it was not speech just yet.

He did not talk or play in a typical manner; he was more of a sorter, building bridges and paths from stacked books on the floor. Christian appeared apathetic about most things other than screens: screens of computers, televisions, tablets, and Leapster controls.

However, he did go online and interact with Elmo's World on the Sesame Street websites. He would perch on my lap at the computer desk, and we'd learn our letters.

But when 'Blue's Clues' was on, he would get so excited and shout, "It's over there!" to Joe or Steve when the clue was dancing on the screen.

While First Steps did wonders for Christian, the process was initially unpleasant. The older intake gentleman who met Christian arranged with us what experts were needed and delivered some harsh truths or rather assumptions.

While I realize now that the man was attempting to be realistic with me about my child, it was hard hearing, "Your child might not comprehend certain things. Like you're his mother and you love him. That might not be something he'll ever understand. Love is something he may not be able to do."

During the sessions with each specialist, I would stare at them, monitoring their full session, because rarely—rarely, did I ever allow someone to take on the role of full caregiver even for an hour or so.

In hindsight, I am certain I made these wonderful ladies work miracles on making my son uncomfortable. I just did not want them to parent my child because in case of a meltdown which consisted of behavior that would typically scare people like watching my baby throw his tiny body into walls, hard brick walls.

I also watched them in order to replicate those sessions, so we can continue to make the progress necessary for my baby to communicate and function in a socially appropriate way.

The OT suggested a weighted blanket, a brushing technique with joint compressions called the *Wilbarger Protocol*, and access to movement activities like a trampoline because Christian's meltdowns and other sensory-seeking behavior indicated that he is seeking pressure impact to engage his nervous system.

He liked being squished and squeezed like Temple Grandin's squeeze machine.

Christian was diagnosed or identified as pervasive development disorder until he was seven years old which allowed him to receive services through special education through this label.

But afterward, he did get a medical diagnoses of autism, a word that I put off, put aside, delayed as much as possible. The word autism was scary. It was the *point of no return* scary. It meant a much more permanent situation for my son, a cognitive disability.

The more I learned, the more I realized that autism looks like all kinds of different things because it is a spectrum. Christian cognitive abilities were strong, as was his ability to empathize, a skill normally foreign to those on the spectrum.

But like I said—not always. Something true for one person with autism is not true for another person with autism.

At the time, we lived in Richmond, Kentucky. As we enrolled Christian into school, I met with a very unusual teacher who seemed to be past her prime, a bit of an old crow, grumpy with noise and did not appear to be on board with Christian's situation like she did not believe him, or us for that matter.

When we shared with her our recommendations from First Steps, there were strange comments made: like how an OT should not be making a physical therapist's recommendations like a trampoline, and a few side comments about *just correct him.* As though everything my baby boy was dealing with was bad parenting of a disobedient child.

We left the enrollment meeting deciding to wait to enroll Christian in Wilmore, Kentucky, where we moved.

While the schools in Wilmore were filled with caring and competent educators, all the IEP meetings I attended made me feel dumb. I had finished my master's degree in Richmond and started my adjunct position at the local university, but still, I felt dumb.

I don't know if you know this but teachers—WE TALK FUNNY! We speak in these TLAs (Three-Letter Acronyms).

These angelic elementary school teachers would process the paperwork with me, where I continued to process all that my son was not able to do, what continued to make him different, and what made things hard for him. And I could barely follow the conversation.

It was at these mystifying meetings that I made the decision that I needed to add a special education endorsement to my Alternative Education certification so I could be the best mom and advocate for my baby boy.

The study of special education put a sacredness to what I was doing. I would learn about sped law, why it was important, why those deadlines mattered, and how it was all tied back to student rights and the parents' ability to advocate for the rights and accessibility of education for their children.

That's when I learned the magic term FAPE—Free Appropriate Public Education. It's a civil rights law protecting student access to education regardless of whether they are in a wheelchair or struggling to function socially throughout the school day which is all part of IDEA—Individuals with Disabilities Act.

After I finished my degree, I was ready to climb out from under my rock and see more than cattle and factories, so, my family and I were like 'Heads Carolina' and headed north to Alaska.

It is a grave sin to move away from one's family down in the holler. In some families, women were given family property when they were married, and families started their own little family villages off the same property sectioned off for each family member.

While I am not from the holler nor is this practice a thing in my own life, my mother was given a little plot off Richie Lane that she somehow lost during my custody battle. I am not sure how/what happened, but all that to say, there is a long history where I come from of sticking with family.

In the book *Whistling and Crowing*, one subject said, "I'd rather have poverty of wealth than a poverty of spirit," when discussing why she chose to stay in the land of no opportunity.

It reminds me of a conversation I had with my mom many years ago. She was complaining about my dad's family. She said, "You can tell how close your daddy's family is by the distance they live from each other. How much farther can people get from each other…California to Kentucky."

As I stand on my deck of the little blue house with the yellow door, overlooking the water of Narrows, I consider what my mother said and think to myself, *how much farther? Hold my beer!*

There is a sense of freedom in movement, all types of movement, whether it be place to place, on foot, on wheels, or lifted into the air. The very movement, the motion, itself becomes therapeutic.

Movement, especially with a strong breeze, is like flight. In the car, with the windows down, music loud, and feeling the wind through my hair as I drive slightly faster than I should is like flight. Gliding on roller skates is flight.

Sort of like learning to walk, I don't remember learning to skate since my first daycare was a roller rink. But I remember the joy of it. The floating, gliding, the flight. There is really nothing like flight. My husband and I took the kids to North Carolina with his parents.

We took the kids to see the Wright Brothers Museum and I got to fly Jockey's Ridge which is a big hot sand dune that could be hiding sea glass broken down and discarded years ago during Prohibition, when they hid liquor in the sand dunes.

Jockey's Ridge was also one of the places the Wright Brothers attempted flight. Our guide had us all by a kite string when we took our turn on the hang glider made of white heavy canvas stretched out over a metal frame. The feeling of being lifted by the gigantic human-sized kite is exhilarating.

First, you feel weightless as you are lifted into the air. Then, you feel the breeze catch and hold you in the air. Finally, the kite lowers as you head toward the bottom sloping dune and drops in a pillow of hot sand. That. That is freedom.